Becoming You

Sabyasachi Ghosh

Contents

Foreword

Some books are loud. Some books are smart and then there are books that feel like a soft whisper in the dark, just when you need it most.

This is one of those books.

I didn't write *Becoming You* from a mountaintop. I wrote it from the middle of my own storms on nights when I felt lost, invisible, or quietly broken. I was not trying to impress the world. I was simply trying to understand myself.

And maybe... to speak to someone out there who feels the same.

You might be that person. If you've ever questioned your worth, doubted your strength, or felt like the world moved too fast while you were still healing, this book is for you. If you've carried silent pain, tried to fix yourself quietly, or wondered why your heart feels heavier than your body, this book is for you. You don't need to be perfect to start. You don't need to be fearless to grows and you don't need to have it all figured out to begin again.Through stories, science, Indian wisdom, and honest reflections, *Becoming You* will not tell you who to be. Instead, it will remind you of who you already are beneath the noise which is whole, enough, and incredibly alive.

FOREWORD

I wrote this book for the version of me who needed it years ago. And now I offer it to you with every page carrying a piece of my heart, my hope, and my healing. Take your time with it. Mark your favorite lines. Cry if you need to. Smile when something clicks and above all know this - **You are not behind. You are becoming.**

Preface

Sometimes, the most powerful stories are not loud. They begin in silence when the world is sleeping, and your heart is quietly asking, *"Is there more to life than this?"*

This book was born in one of those moments.

For the last **six months**, I've been writing *Becoming You* with everything I had - my time, my energy, my heart. I didn't just write it from my desk. I wrote it from my real life. From the long nights I couldn't sleep, from the quiet moments I cried alone, and from the small victories that gave me hope again.

I read hundreds of articles, research papers, ancient wisdom, and stories from around the world. But more than that, I listened to myself, to others, and to the little voice inside that kept saying, *"Maybe this could help someone."*

I didn't write this book because I'm perfect or always positive. I wrote it because I know how it feels to be lost. To feel small. To wonder if your dreams are too big, or your pain too heavy.

So if you've ever felt tired but kept going...
If you've ever smiled through a storm...

If you've ever wished someone could just *understand* you. Then this book is for you.

So thank you for picking up this book, for trusting these words, and for letting me walk with you for a while. I may not know your name, but I believe in your heart. You are not behind. You are evolving.

With all my love and warmth,

Sabyasachi Ghosh

Acknowledgments

Writing this book has been one of the most emotional journeys of my life not because I had all the answers, but because I dared to look within and ask the hardest questions. I could never have written these pages alone. So, with folded hands and a full heart, I thank the people who walked beside me knowingly or unknowingly and helped me become who I am. First, I thank Ma and Baba, for believing in me even when I didn't believe in myself. To my Didi and Diptesh Da, your warmth and presence in my life have made even the darkest days feel a little lighter. To my Dada and Boudidi, your quiet strength and encouragement have always been my guiding light. To Monima and Jathababa, your faith in me is a blessing. To Majjathu, your encouragement and faith gave me the courage to keep moving forward. To my Sensei, your guidance and wisdom have been a beacon of light on my path. Your teachings taught me discipline, patience, and the power of quiet strength and last but not the list to all the friends, mentors, teachers, and strangers who crossed my path and left behind a lesson, I carry your wisdom with me in every chapter of this book. To the startup world, where I discovered how much pressure a heart can take, and how much strength it can build in return, thank you for shaping me. To the books, myths, research papers, and ancient stories that told truths when I needed them most, you are the invisible co-authors of this book. And finally, to you, my reader, this book was written for you. Every word, every example, every page was created with the hope that it reaches your soul. I may not know your name, but I believe in your story. Thank you for giving me space in your life, I will never take that for granted. This book is my offering to the world. But its heartbeat... is made of everyone I just mentioned. Thank you all!

Prologue

This book didn't begin with a plan. It wasn't outlined in a notebook or brainstormed on a whiteboard. It began with a quiet ache, a feeling I couldn't ignore. A deep, gentle question that echoed within me during late nights and early mornings: *"Is this really all there is? Or is there something more I'm meant to become?"* That question stayed with me, followed me through the ordinary days and the restless nights, and slowly grew into a journey, one that would change me from the inside out.

For the past **six months**, I've lived this book. I didn't write it as someone who has everything figured out. I wrote it as someone who was willing to ask hard questions, sit with uncomfortable truths, and walk through the messiness of life with open eyes and an open heart. *Becoming You* was built from real, personal experiences - the kind that leave quiet scars and powerful lessons. I've also grounded it in deep research, pulling from psychology, neuroscience, ancient wisdom, spiritual truths, and the everyday insights that show up when we pause and pay attention to life. I spent hours reading, reflecting, and listening not just to books and studies, but to people. Real people. Their struggles, their hopes, their fears. People who were doing their best to hold themselves together while the world expected them to shine.

This book is not a manual. It's not a list of rules or success formulas. You won't find any shouting motivation or rigid steps here. What you will find is a soft light, a quiet companion to walk with you during the days when your own light feels dim. I wrote this for the ones who feel like they're falling behind. For the dreamers who are still stuck at the starting line. For the high achievers who've checked every box but still feel empty. For the gentle souls who are always strong for others, but silently break when they're alone.

If you've ever smiled to avoid questions, if you've ever cried quietly so no one would worry, if you've ever doubted your worth, your pace, your voice - this book is for you. It doesn't promise to fix your life, but it will remind you that you were never broken to begin with. It will tell you what the world forgets to say: that your softness is strength, your slowness is not failure, and your presence exactly as it is more than enough. Because you are not behind. You are not too late. You are not too much, or not enough. You are *becoming*.

And what you're becoming is not just beautiful. It's necessary. The world needs more people who are honest, gentle, and awake to their own light. This book is a celebration of that light, the one that's always been inside you, waiting patiently to be remembered.

1. The Ordinary Beginning

Have you ever looked at the sky just before sunrise?

It's not loud. It doesn't rush. It takes its time to slowly spreading color into darkness. That's how ordinary lives become extraordinary. Not with noise. But with patience. You see, most of us are taught to chase big things. Big dreams, big success, big money. But no one tells us the secret, the real magic is hidden in small things. In how you treat a stranger. In how you talk to yourself on hard days. In how you keep showing up, even when no one is clapping for you. When I was a child, no one told me I was going to be special. And that's okay. Because the truth is, I didn't need to be special. I needed to be *real.* I needed to be *present.* That's what saved me.

I remember once sitting outside my school in Bhangar. It was raining. My slippers were soaked, my uniform muddy. I didn't feel like a future engineer or a writer. I just felt... small. But then, a teacher walked past me and said, "You're still here?" I nodded, embarrassed. He smiled and said, "Good. Staying is the first sign of strength."

That moment never left me. It taught me something powerful, being ordinary is not about being weak. It's about standing in the rain when it's easier to run. You may not win every time. People may ignore you. Life may delay your dreams. But don't let the world rush you into believing you're late. You're not late. You're learning, Growing and Becoming. I know people who never topped their class but now run their own businesses. I've seen students who failed in school become the best teachers of life. Because life doesn't check your report card. It checks your *resilience.* So if you're reading this with doubts in your heart. I want you to know this: You are not a background character. You are the author of your own story. And every little moment even the boring ones are building by you. One day, someone will look at you and say, "How did you become so strong?" And you'll smile gently and say, "I stayed." Stayed through the storms. Stayed through the silence. Stayed when everything inside me wanted to quit. That's the power of ordinary beginnings. They turn into legendary stories , one quiet step at a time. There's a strange truth about success. It often wears the disguise of failure in the beginning.

In 1997, a woman named Joanne was divorced, broke, and raising a child on government support. She sat in cafés, scribbling words on napkins while her baby slept beside her. Publishers rejected her book twelve times. But she didn't stop. She couldn't. The world now knows her as **J.K. Rowling**. And her story *"Harry Potter" became* a beacon for millions. But before the magic, there was mess. Before Hogwarts, there was heartbreak. Why does this matter? Because the most extraordinary stories almost always begin in ordinary chaos. The people who change the world are not born with perfect lives and they are shaped by imperfect moments. Research from Harvard University shows that people who experience small, consistent struggles early in life, not massive trauma, but modest hardship often develop what psychologists call "**grit**." Grit is a better predictor of long-term success than IQ or talent. It's the stubborn spirit that whispers, "Don't give up yet," when everything else tells you to quit. So when you feel behind, or broken, or lost , remember: you are building grit.

I often smile at the memory of my own silent struggles like walking miles to attend classes, sharing one computer with ten students, dreaming big while surviving small. Those days didn't make me weaker. They made me real. They taught me to be grateful for the little I had, and hungry for the more I believed I could create. Let me ask you something: When was the last time you celebrated yourself for not giving up? We clap when someone wins, but what about the days they simply *continued?* The world's slowest-growing plant, the **Puya raimondii** in the Andes, takes *80 years* to bloom once but when it does, it's magnificent. Maybe your life is like that too. Maybe you're not late, maybe you're preparing for a rare kind of greatness. Every morning you rise despite the weight on your shoulders, you're becoming someone the world has never seen before. Not because you were born special. But because you chose not to sink when life got heavy. The people who leave the deepest marks in this world are not always the loudest. They are the ones who walk quietly but refuse to stop walking. So if you're reading this feeling average, or invisible, or unfinished remember this one truth:

Extraordinary lives are just ordinary lives, deeply lived.

And your beginning, however plain it looks now, is glowing with unseen promise. Have you ever felt like your life is too small to make a big difference? Let me share something amazing. In Japan, there is a concept called **"ikigai"**. It means "a reason for being." It's not about fame or money. It's about waking up in the morning with purpose. It could be as simple as making your child smile, cooking for your family, or finishing one page of your dream project. People in a small island in Japan called **Okinawa** live the longest in the world, and many researchers believe it's because they follow ikigai. They live ordinary lives with deep meaning. This proves something important. You don't need to be famous to be fulfilled. You just need purpose.

Let me tell you another true story.

There was once a janitor who worked at NASA in the 1960s. One day, President John F. Kennedy visited the NASA space center. He saw the janitor sweeping the floor and asked, "What are you doing here?" The janitor replied, "I'm helping put a man on the moon." Just imagine that. He didn't say, "I'm cleaning floors."

He saw himself as part of something greater. That's what purpose does. It transforms even the smallest task into something powerful. You don't have to change the whole world. You just have to change how you *see* the world. Even in my own life, I've noticed, when I saw my work as just "work," it felt heavy. But when I saw it as service, as something that might help someone someday, it started to feel lighter. Even joyful.

Science says: A study by Yale researchers showed that people who see their jobs as a calling, not just a way to earn money are *happier*, healthier, and more satisfied in life. It doesn't matter what you do. It matters **why** do you do it. Your reason can be anything. To care for your family. To become better than yesterday. To prove to your younger self that you didn't give up.

You don't need a loud beginning. You need a loving one. You may not see it now, but even your daily struggles like catching a bus, studying late, cooking for others, working while tired they are not wasted.

They are the quiet building blocks of a strong, meaningful life.

So, the next time you feel "just ordinary," pause. Smile.
Remind yourself: The light inside you may be small, but it's steady. And one day, it will guide others out of their darkness too. Have you ever watched how a river flows? It doesn't complain when it hits a rock. It bends. It curves. It slows down. But it never stops. Life is like that river. And you, you're flowing even on the days you think you're stuck. You might feel like you're not moving fast enough. You might think others are ahead of you in career, in love, in life. The secret most people never tell you:

Growth is not always visible.

A tree spends years growing roots before it ever shows a leaf. A caterpillar dissolves completely before it becomes a butterfly. Even the moon disappears for a while but it always comes back full that means even when your life feels slow, quiet, or invisible, something deep inside you is changing. There's a term in psychology called **"The Invisible Progress Curve."** It's the idea that progress doesn't happen like a straight line. At first, you may try and try, and see no result. But suddenly, after weeks or months, things click. This is how people learn a new language, build a habit or heal from pain.

Let me give you a fun example from nature. Do you know how **bamboo grows**?

For the first **five years**, you water it daily and see nothing. Just soil. But in the **sixth year**, it suddenly grows **90 feet in just six weeks**. So what was it doing all those years? It was growing roots which is deep, strong roots to support its future. Maybe that's what you're doing now. Building invisible strength.

When I was studying computer science, there were moments I thought, "What's the point?" I didn't see instant rewards. Others seemed to shine while I struggled silently. But now I realize I was planting roots. Roots of patience, discipline, and resilience. No one claps when you're building roots. But that's okay. Because roots are not for others to see, they're for you to stand strong when storms come. So if today feels slow, or hard, or quiet, trust the roots. You are not failing. You are preparing. You are growing, even when no one sees it. Because one day, just like the bamboo, you will rise and those who once doubted your silence will be surprised by your strength.

There's something quietly powerful about what you do when no one is watching. The world generally celebrates the big wins like awards, promotions, achievements. But behind every shining moment are thousands of quiet ones. Early mornings. Lonely evenings. Small habits. Moments where you could have chosen comfort, but instead, you chose effort.

And that's what builds you.

A study from **Stanford University** revealed something fascinating: people who believe that discipline is more important than motivation are more consistent in reaching their goals. Motivation comes and goes but habits, once formed, hold you like roots under the earth.

So don't wait to feel inspired every day. Instead, build a rhythm even a soft one. Wake up and read one page. Write one sentence. Do five minutes of learning. Drink a glass of water with intention. Smile at someone who didn't expect it.

These may feel too small to matter. But they do. In Japan, there's a philosophy called **Kaizen**, the practice of continuous, small improvements. Even 1% better every day adds up to **37 times** better in a year. That's not just math, it's magic. Your future doesn't arrive all at once. It grows gently in the shadow of today's small acts.

Let me tell you a story from real life.

When **Will Smith**, one of the most successful actors of our time, was a boy, his father asked him and his brother to build a brick wall. Day after day, brick by brick, they worked under the sun. It took over a year. When they finished, his father said, "Don't ever tell me you can't do something. You just built a wall." Will later said, *"You don't try to build a wall. You lay* *one brick as perfectly as you can. And then you do that again, and again, and again.*" This story stayed with me for years. Because I, too, have laid my bricks in silence, in hope, in faith. Every page of this book is a brick. Every choice you make today is a brick and someday, without realizing it, you'll turn around and see a strong, beautiful life standing behind you made of small days, lived with great love.

So don't rush. Don't compare. Lay your brick and when life feels slow, tell yourself this: "I am not behind. I am building."

One of the quietest thieves of happiness is comparison. It sneaks in without warning. A glance at someone's success story online, a whispered word at work, a friend's sudden good news. Suddenly, your own journey feels small, slow, or not enough.

But a truth that many forget:

Comparison is a thief. It steals joy, peace, and momentum.

Science has proven that our brains are wired to compare, a survival skill from ancient times, when we needed to know who was stronger or faster to survive. But today, this ancient habit often traps us in a cycle of doubt and frustration. Psychologists call this "social comparison theory," and it explains why scrolling through social media can make people feel worse about themselves, even when their lives are good. So what do we do when comparison strikes? The answer is simple, but powerful:

Turn inward, not outward.

Focus on your own light, your own path. Always, remember everyone's life is a unique story, with different challenges, timing, and gifts. Even the tallest tree in the forest started as a tiny seed. Its growth was slow and hidden beneath the soil before it touched the sky. When you catch yourself comparing, pause. Take a deep breath.Remind yourself that your journey is yours alone. This small practice, repeated daily, rewires your brain toward gratitude and self-compassion. Studies show that practicing gratitude reduces stress, improves mental health, and boosts resilience. It doesn't erase struggles, but it changes how you face them with strength and calm. One of my favorite ways to practice this is to write down **three small wins** each day. They can be as simple as waking up early, helping a friend, or learning a new word. Over time, these small wins build a fortress of confidence and peace inside you. So instead of looking left or right, Look straight ahead toward your own quiet, steady light. Your progress is real, your effort matters and your story is worthy. The world doesn't need another copy of someone else. It needs the original you and that original you has a light that never leaves. Throughout history, some of the greatest successes were born from failure. Thomas Edison, the inventor of the light bulb, famously said,

"I have not failed. I've just found 10,000 ways that won't work." His unwavering curiosity and resilience transformed repeated failure into a spark that lit up the world. Psychologists explain this phenomenon through the idea of ***"growth mindset,"*** a term popularized by Dr. Carol Dweck. People with a this mindset believe that abilities and intelligence can be developed through dedication and hard work. They view failure not as a permanent setback, but as feedback a necessary part of learning and growing.

Research shows that accepting failure can increase creativity, deepen learning, and build emotional strength. Our brains actually change when we face challenges and setbacks. Every time you try, fail, and try again, you are literally rewiring your brain to become stronger. This doesn't mean failure is easy to accept. It hurts. It disappoints. But it also invites you to reflect, adjust, and move forward with wiser steps. Sometimes, the most painful moments are the ones that teach us the most about who we truly are. When I faced moments of failure during my studies or work, I learned to ask myself, "What can this teach me?" instead of "Why did this happen to me?" That shift in question changed everything. It gave me courage to try again, to grow, and to keep laying my bricks quietly.

So, Failure is not the end. It is a bend in the road, a challenge that shapes your journey. Every great story includes failures they are the shadows that make the light shine brighter. Keep your head high, Keep your heart open and keep walking. Because the light inside you that never leaves is waiting to shine through. Research by psychologist reveals two main types of mindset: the fixed mindset and the growth mindset. A fixed mindset believes abilities are fixed traits, you are either born smart or you aren't. It fears failure and avoids challenges, because any misstep feels like proof of inadequacy. On the other hand, a it sees abilities as skills that can be nurtured through effort and learning. It welcomes challenges, embraces mistakes as lessons, and keeps pushing forward. The good news is, mindset is not fixed. It's like a muscle, the more you exercise it, the stronger it becomes. Small daily habits of reflection, gratitude, and self-talk can help shift your mindset toward growth. Studies show that people with a growth mindset are more resilient, more creative, and more successful in their personal and professional lives. They are also kinder to themselves in moments of struggle, which is vital for long-term well-being. This doesn't mean you have to be perfect. It means you are willing to keep trying, learning, and evolving.

Your mindset will shape how you respond to life's tests. Will you see obstacles as walls or as doors? Will you give up or will you keep laying bricks, one after another? Remember, the light inside you that never leaves is fueled by your mindset. Cultivate it. Protect it. And watch how your life begins to change, not overnight, but steadily, quietly, beautifully. Your mindset is the way you see the world. It shapes how you think about yourself, your problems, and your chances to grow. Mindset is not just about being positive or hopeful. It is a deep way you understand life and what happens to you. Habits are the small actions we do every day — often without thinking. Yet, these tiny actions quietly shape who we become and how we feel. Imagine habits as the bricks that build the house of your mindset and your life. Scientists say that most of what we do each day is controlled by habits. This means the way we react, think, and behave is often automatic. The good news is, if we choose to create healthy and positive habits, they become powerful tools to grow our mindset and happiness. For example, waking up early, writing down things you are thankful for, or reading a few pages of a good book may seem small. But when done daily, they change your brain and your attitude. Research in psychology shows that simple habits like these increase our focus, reduce stress, and help us feel more in control. But changing habits isn't easy. It takes time and patience. The brain loves routines and will resist new habits at first. This is normal. The key is to start small and keep going, even if you miss a day or two. Every effort counts.

When I started working on my own habits, I began with writing three good things that happened each day. It helped me notice the light even on dark days. Little by little, these moments built a stronger mindset and more peace inside me. Your habits can become your strongest allies or your biggest obstacles. Choose them wisely. Build habits that support your growth, kindness, and courage. Remember, the light inside you that never leaves is nourished by what you do every day. The small choices you make now will shape your life's story like one page, one habit, one moment at a time. Change often feels like something huge and far away like a big event or a sudden miracle. But the truth is, real change usually happens quietly, through small, consistent actions repeated day after day. This idea is not just a motivational phrase; it is backed by science.

In 2009, a study by psychologist Dr. Phillippa Lally and her team followed hundreds of people as they tried to form new habits. They found that, on average, it takes about 66 days — more than two months of doing something regularly before it becomes automatic. This means if you want to build a habit like daily reading, exercising, or practicing gratitude, it will take time and patience. What's even more fascinating is how these small habits add up over time, like drops of water filling a jar. One day, you look back and realize you have built strength, calmness, or skill without even noticing it happening day to day. This is called *compound effect*, small changes that grow into big results.

Another powerful idea comes from the world of neuroscience. When you repeat an action regularly, your brain forms new pathways, called *neural circuits.* These circuits make the action easier and faster each time. That is why practice makes perfect not because you suddenly become a genius, but because your brain is rewiring itself. The challenge is staying consistent. Life throws distractions, doubts, and obstacles in the way. But even if you miss a day or face setbacks, the key is to return without giving up. Research shows that self-compassion. Being kind to yourself when things don't go perfectly, it helps people keep going and build lasting change. In my own life, I've experienced how small steps, taken patiently and with kindness, create lasting growth. When I was learning new skills or facing tough times, focusing on one simple habit like deep breathing or positive thinking made my journey manageable and hopeful. So, as you walk your path, remember this: you don't need to change everything at once. Start with one small, positive action. Do it daily. Trust the process. Your light inside will grow stronger with every gentle step you take. The place where we live, the people around us, and even the sounds and smells we notice every day. All of these shape the person we are becoming. Our environment acts like an invisible guide, gently pushing us toward certain habits, thoughts, and feelings. Scientific studies show that our surroundings influence up to 40% of our behaviors without us even realizing it. This means the people we spend time with, the spaces we choose to be in, and the things we see every day quietly affect our mindset and mood.

For example, researchers at Duke University found that when people surround themselves with positive, motivated friends, they are more likely to succeed in their own goals. On the other hand, being in negative or stressful environments can make it harder to grow and stay hopeful. It's not just about people, but also about the physical space. Cluttered, noisy, or dark places can increase stress and drain energy. Simple changes like cleaning your room, opening windows to let in sunlight, or adding plants can brighten your mind and soul. Our brains love order and light they help us feel calm and focused. When I was studying or working, I noticed how much my surroundings mattered. Quiet, clean spaces helped me think better, while distractions made it hard to focus. So, I started to choose where I worked and how I arranged my things carefully. You don't need a perfect place. Even small changes like playing soft music, lighting a candle, or keeping a photo of someone you love nearby can lift your spirit and remind you of your inner strength. Remember, the light inside you that never leaves shines brightest when your environment supports your growth. Choose your surroundings like you choose your thoughts — with care and kindness. This is why creating a safe, positive space around you is one of the first steps in your journey of self-help. It is the soil where the seeds of your habits, mindset, and dreams can grow strong and tall. The stories we tell ourselves are some of the most powerful forces in our lives. From early childhood, we begin to create a narrative, a personal story about who we are, what we can do, and what life expects from us. These stories shape our beliefs and actions more than we often realize.

Psychologists call this our *self-narrative*. It's like the script we follow every day. If the story says, "I am not good enough" or "I always fail," then our actions often match that belief. But if we tell ourselves, "I am learning and growing," or "I can overcome challenges," our minds start to work in new, hopeful ways. Research shows that when people rewrite their self-narrative with kindness and truth, they become more resilient and confident. This idea is called *narrative therapy*, where changing the story changes the person's life. In my own journey, I found that many of my fears and doubts came from old stories that were not really true. I remember thinking, "I am just an ordinary person; I will never do anything special." But over time, I began to tell myself a new story. One where effort and hope mattered more than perfection. This simple change helped me face difficulties with courage and kindness. Your story is yours to write. No one else holds the pen. You can choose to let old, limiting beliefs fade and create a new story that lifts you up, no matter what has happened before. This does not mean ignoring pain or pretending everything is perfect. It means seeing your struggles as part of a bigger, meaningful story, a story where you are the hero growing stronger with every step. The light inside you that never leaves shines brightest when your story is filled with hope, truth, and love. Choose your words wisely. Speak kindly to yourself. And watch how your world begins to change. Many people think emotions are something to avoid or control tightly. We are taught to hide sadness, anger, or fear. But emotions are not enemies. They are messages — signals from inside us that tell a deeper story.

Science teaches us that emotions evolved to help humans survive. Fear warns us of danger; sadness asks us to rest and heal; anger shows us where boundaries are crossed. When we listen carefully, emotions guide us toward what we need to grow. For example, studies in psychology reveal that accepting and naming emotions instead of pushing them away leads to better mental health. This practice, called *emotional awareness*, helps calm the mind and body. It allows us to respond wisely instead of reacting with fear or anger. I remember times when I was overwhelmed by difficult feelings. At first, I tried to ignore them. But later, I learned to sit quietly, breathe deeply, and gently ask myself, "What is this feeling trying to tell me?" That simple question opened a door to understanding and healing. Emotions are like a compass for the heart. When you learn to read them kindly, they help you navigate life's storms and find peace. The light inside you that never leaves shines brightest when you honor your feelings with love and patience. Don't fight your emotions. Invite them in. Learn from them. And you will grow stronger and wiser every day. Many people think emotions are something to avoid or control tightly. We are taught to hide sadness, anger, or fear. But emotions are not enemies. They are messages which is the signals from inside us that tell a deeper story.

Pause for a moment. When you feel sad or angry, do you try to push those feelings away? Or do you try to understand what they might be saying?

Science teaches us that emotions evolved to help humans survive. Fear warns us of danger; sadness asks us to rest and heal; anger shows us where boundaries are crossed. When we listen carefully, emotions guide us toward what we need to grow.

Think about a recent time when you felt overwhelmed. Did you allow yourself to feel the emotion fully, or did you try to ignore it? What happened afterward?

Patience is one of the quietest, yet most powerful companions on the path of growth. In a world that rushes forward, where instant results are expected, patience feels almost like a lost art. But real transformation asks for time and gentle waiting.

Science tells us that the brain needs repeated practice over weeks and months to build new habits and ways of thinking. The neurons that fire together, wire together — this process doesn't happen overnight. It's slow, steady, and sometimes frustrating.

Ask yourself: How patient have you been with yourself when trying to change? Have you given up too soon? Or have you allowed your journey the time it needs?

Along with patience, self-forgiveness is a lifeline. When we stumble or fall short, harsh self-judgment only deepens pain and blocks progress. Researchers in psychology have shown that people who practice self-forgiveness recover faster from failures and have better emotional health. I learned this truth the hard way. There were moments when I was my own worst critic, condemning myself for mistakes. But when I started speaking kindly to myself saying, "It's okay to be human, it's okay to make mistakes". I felt a warmth and strength I hadn't known before.

Think now: What words of kindness can you offer yourself when things don't go as planned?

Growth is not a race but a steady unfolding. The light inside you that never leaves glows strongest when wrapped in patience and gentle forgiveness. These are not signs of weakness, but of deep courage.

Sometimes we wait for a big moment to change our lives. A sudden success, a huge opportunity, or a life-changing event. But most of the time, our future is shaped not by one grand act, but by hundreds of small choices we make every day. Every morning you wake up is a fresh chance. What you choose to think, say, and do even in the smallest ways slowly carves the direction of your life. This idea may sound simple, but research in behavioral science backs it. Tiny, repeated actions create strong patterns in the brain over time. For example, choosing to walk instead of staying in bed, reading a few pages of a helpful book, drinking water instead of a sugary drink, or even simply taking a deep breath when stressed, these are not tiny acts. They are powerful votes for the personYou're unfolding.

What kind of person do you want to be a year from now? What daily action could you begin today to move in that direction?

I used to think greatness came from doing something heroic. But now I know, it often comes from doing the ordinary things with care, every single day. The light inside you becomes brighter not in one flash, but through the steady glow of consistent steps. You don't need to climb a mountain today. You just need to take the next honest step. And then another. Have you ever noticed how powerful words can be? A few kind words from someone can lift your whole day and a few harsh ones even if they come from yourself can stay in your mind for weeks. We often think words are just sound, but they carry energy. They shape how we think, feel, and live.

What we say to others is important. But what we say to ourselves is even more powerful. Sometimes, we carry words from the past things someone once said to us. Maybe they told you that you weren't good enough, or that your dreams were foolish. Even if those words were said years ago, they can live quietly in our minds and hold us back. But the truth is, you don't have to believe everything you've heard. You can choose new words. Gentle ones. Strong ones. Honest ones. Words that lift you up, not tear you down.

What if you started speaking to yourself the way you would speak to someone you truly love?

I remember standing in front of a mirror once, feeling broken and small. Then I looked into my own eyes and said, "I'm proud of you for not giving up." It felt strange at first but then, something inside me softened. I started saying things like, "You're trying your best," or, "You're allowed to grow slowly." And slowly, I began to heal.

Your words are like seeds. Whatever you plant will grow. Plant kindness. Plant hope. Plant courage. Let this be the beginning of a new way to speak not just to the world, but to yourself. Gentleness is often misunderstood. People think it means weakness. Being soft, slow, or silent. But gentleness is one of the strongest forces in the world. It takes real strength to stay calm when you could explode, to show kindness when you're hurt, and to choose peace when your heart is on fire. Think about water. It's soft, it flows, it bends. But over time, it can carve through mountains. That's the power of gentleness is steady, silent, and unstoppable. In life, many situations test our patience. People may misunderstand us, disappoint us, or treat us unfairly. It's easy to react with anger or blame. But gentleness teaches us to breathe, to pause, and to respond with grace. It doesn't mean we allow harm. It means we handle it without letting it change who we are inside. Some of the strongest people you'll ever meet are those who speak softly, listen deeply, and walk away from fights they could have won just to protect their peace. I've learned that gentle people feel deeply. They cry in silence. They smile through pain. But they don't give up on goodness. Their strength is quiet, but it builds a kind of trust that noise can never buy. In your own journey, never be ashamed of being gentle. Never believe that kindness makes you less powerful. The world needs more calm voices, more warm hands, and more people who know how to love without shouting. Be soft. But don't be weak. Let your gentleness be your courage.Every day begins in silence. Before the noise, before the world wakes up there's a quiet invitation in the morning air. It says, "You can start again."

No matter what happened yesterday, no matter how heavy the past may feel, today is new. The sun rises without asking who failed or who succeeded. It just shines like it always does. We often carry old memories, regrets, and pain as if they are part of who we are. But the truth is, we are not our worst days. We are not our past mistakes. We are what we choose to become now. Life gives us more than one chance. It gives us one every morning. This is the gift most people overlook, the power to begin again, slowly, quietly, with courage. I've had days when I didn't feel like getting out of bed. Days when hope felt far away. But still, somehow, I managed to take one small step. And sometimes, that was enough. Not to fix everything, but to remind myself that healing begins with movement, not perfection. No one starts life as an expert. We all begin as learners with shaking hands, unsure steps, and dreams that feel bigger than we can hold. But we grow. We fall. We rise again. And in that cycle, we learn who we really are. The beginning is never behind you. It's always beside you, waiting. In a breath. In a choice. In a moment of bravery. So even if today feels like a mess, even if nothing makes sense, start again. Not because it's easy. But because deep inside, you still believe there's more waiting for you and you're right. Pain changes people. It doesn't ask for permission. It doesn't knock politely. It walks in without warning and rearranges everything inside us. And yet, somehow, pain also reveals what truly matters.

There are moments in life when the world seems to go quiet not in peace, but in shock. You sit with your pain, not knowing what to do with it. It can feel like an invisible weight pressing on your chest, like a sadness that doesn't always come with tears. Some people will notice. Many won't. But you feel it deeply and that's enough to change you. Pain, when faced with honesty, teaches us things we never learn in comfort. It shows us who we are underneath all the layers. It teaches us about strength, not the kind that shouts, but the kind that whispers, "I'm still here." The strange thing is, people who've known pain often carry more compassion. They notice the silent battles in others. They become gentler. More forgiving. More real. Their smiles are softer. Their words are slower. They understand without needing all the details. You don't have to be proud of the pain you've been through. But you can be proud of how you carried it. You can be proud of how you held yourself together when everything was falling apart. That kind of quiet bravery matters. What hurt you did not end you. It changed you. And sometimes, that change becomes the birthplace of a softer heart, a wiser soul, and a deeper purpose. So if today you feel broken, remember some things grow better after being broken. Like muscles that grow after pressure. Like pottery repaired with gold. Like people who shine not because they were never hurt, but because they survived and still chose love and that is something powerful. We often live in places we cannot touch, the past that haunts us, or the future that scares us. But life only happens in one moment: now.

Right now, as your eyes move across these words, something sacred is taking place. You are breathing. Your heart is beating. Your mind is awake. This moment, simple as it seems, is the only place where life exists.

The past is already written. We cannot walk backward. The future is still a mystery. We cannot live in a time that hasn't arrived. But the present, this moment is where change, love, courage, and healing begin. So often, we rush. We check our phones. We plan endlessly. We worry about what's next. In doing so, we miss the gentle beauty of what's already here — the sound of birds, the warmth of light on our skin, the taste of our food, the feeling of being safe for just one second. Being present doesn't mean everything is perfect. It means we're not lost. It means we're choosing to live instead of merely existing. I used to think I had to fix everything at once. But I learned that one mindful breath, one real smile, one moment of full attention can create more peace than a thousand anxious thoughts. Presence is not passive. It's powerful. It's how we reclaim our life, one moment at a time. So sit with yourself. Feel the weight of your body, the sound around you, the emotions inside you without judging them. Just notice. That's where awareness begins. That's where healing quietly waits.

The moment you return to now, you find something the past can't offer and the future can't promise peace and in peace, we start to remember who we really are. Believing again. It sounds simple, doesn't it? But if you've been broken, if you've trusted and been hurt, if you've hoped and been disappointed, you know how hard it is. It's not the grand betrayals that always shake us the most. Sometimes, it's the small ones: the promises that were never kept, the friends who slowly faded, the dreams we whispered that no one protected. These moments collect silently in our hearts, making it harder to believe in others, in ourselves, in life.

The truth is that the ability to believe again is not a sign of weakness. It's a deep, silent kind of strength. When you choose to open your heart again after being hurt, you are not forgetting the pain and yes you are rising above it. Belief doesn't mean expecting perfection. It means giving life another chance. It means saying, "Maybe this time, things will grow." It's planting seeds even after the last storm took everything away. You don't need to rush. You don't need to shout your belief to the world. Just start with a whisper:
"I believe healing is possible."
"I believe I still matter."
"I believe that good people exist."
"I believe I can try again." and with each soft belief, your soul begins to stretch again. The walls inside you become windows. Light finds a way in. No, you won't forget the past. You're not supposed to but you'll learn that what happened to you doesn't own your future. Your belief is what builds it. Every strong person you admire has one thing in common. They dared to believe again when it would've been easier to stop. That's where strength is born, not in perfection, but in choosing to begin again.

So if today your hands are trembling and your heart is unsure, remember: You're not broken. You're just rebuilding and belief is the first brick. Comparison is a thief that doesn't knock. It sneaks in quietly, sometimes when we're just scrolling, sometimes when we hear about someone else's success. It whispers in our ears, "Look at them. You're falling behind." It's one of the most dangerous traps not because it's loud, but because it's quiet. It hides behind compliments, social media, family expectations, even our own goals. And slowly, it starts to chip away at our peace. You begin to doubt your pace. You question your path. You start thinking that you should be richer, prettier, stronger, smarter more. But "more" never ends. And in chasing it, you forget the beauty of what you already are. The truth is, there is no universal timeline. No single standard for happiness or success. Flowers bloom at different times, and yet each one is beautiful in its own way. Why, then, do we rush our own growth just to match someone else's season? You are not behind. You are not early. You are exactly where you are supposed to be. Your story is not meant to look like anyone else's. It's not supposed to follow the same map.

What if you stopped measuring your worth with someone else's ruler? What if you began to live for your joy, your rhythm, your version of peace? When we stop comparing, something magical happens. We become kinder to ourselves. We start seeing our own strength. We begin to notice how far we've come, not how far we still have to go.

So take a breath and return to your path. Let others run their race. Yours is sacred too. You are not behind. You are becoming. We live in a world obsessed with speed, fast results, fast money, fast answers. But nature doesn't rush, and yet everything it creates is complete. A tree does not become tall overnight. The moon doesn't shine in fullness every night. Healing, growth, and becoming all take time. So why do we punish ourselves for moving slowly? Tiny steps are often invisible to others. They're not loud. They don't always bring applause. But they are powerful. One tiny step can be the difference between giving up and holding on. There's power in the morning you choose to get out of bed even though your heart feels heavy. There's power in the way you speak kindly to yourself after years of self-doubt. There's power in the decision to try again not because everything is okay, but because you are learning to believe it could be. Tiny steps matter. A single drop of water, again and again, can carve a stone. A gentle wind, over time, shapes mountains. That's what consistent, quiet effort looks like. That's what real transformation is. You don't need to make a giant leap today. Just take one small step toward peace. Toward your dream. Toward the version of you who no longer needs to prove anything to anyone not even to yourself. Maybe that step is drinking more water. Maybe it's writing one honest sentence. Maybe it's just letting yourself rest without guilt. Celebrate it.

Every mountain was once a handful of dust. What you do today, no matter how small, builds who you become tomorrow. Keep going at your own pace.

2. The Courage To Feel

— *Sabyasachi Ghosh*

Most of us grow up hearing, "Be strong." But no one tells us what *real* strength looks like. We are taught to hide our pain. To smile even when we're hurting. To say "I'm fine" when inside, we're falling apart. We fear being seen as weak, so we build walls around our hearts. But in truth, this kind of strength is only an illusion.

Real strength is not hiding your feelings. It's having the courage to feel them. Think about this: when we touch a flame, we feel pain instantly. Our body reacts, it protects itself. But when our heart is hurt by words, by rejection, by loneliness, we're told to "move on," to "be tough." But ignoring emotional pain doesn't make us stronger. It only buries the wound deeper. Research in psychology shows that people who allow themselves to feel emotions even the uncomfortable ones like sadness, fear, or anger are healthier in the long run. They don't carry silent pain. They don't explode after years of holding it in. They *heal* because they're honest. It takes deep courage to say, "I'm not okay right now." It takes maturity to admit, "This is hard for me." It takes strength to cry, to open up, to let someone see the real you without masks.

Emotions are not the enemy. They are signals. They tell us what matters. If you're grieving, it means you loved deeply. If you're anxious, it means you care. If you're angry, it means something important to you feels threatened. These are not signs of weakness. These are signs you are *alive*. We often say, "Time heals all wounds." But time alone isn't enough. Feeling heals. Processing heals. Talking heals. Writing heals. Time only gives us space and what we do in that space is what makes healing possible. So today, give yourself permission to feel. Not forever, not all at once just one honest breath at a time. Sit with your emotions like old friends. They're not here to destroy you. They're here to teach you. You are not weak for feeling deeply. You are *human* and that, in itself, is the most powerful thing you could ever be. Strength is often misunderstood. We imagine it as holding everything together, never showing cracks, always standing tall no matter the storm. But real strength is quieter, more subtle. It's the courage to face what we feel, not to hide from it.

Modern science and psychology tell us a powerful truth that suppressing emotions harms us more than expressing them. Studies show that when people bottle up sadness, anger, or fear, they experience more stress, weakened immune systems, and even heart problems. Our bodies and minds are deeply connected, what we hide inside eventually affects us outside. On the other hand, allowing emotions to flow, even painful ones, helps the brain process experiences. This processing reduces anxiety, prevents emotional outbursts, and builds resilience. People who accept their feelings are more self-aware and able to cope with life's challenges in healthier ways. Yet, society often teaches us the opposite. From childhood, many hear, "Don't cry," "Be tough," "Ignore it." These words, though often well-meaning, teach us to build walls — walls that block not only pain but also joy, connection, and healing.

But vulnerability is not weakness. Vulnerability is a doorway, a gateway to genuine connection with ourselves and others. When we allow ourselves to feel fully, we create space for healing to begin. Feeling sadness means we recognize loss; feeling anger means we defend what's important; feeling fear means we acknowledge uncertainty and danger. These feelings are signals, not problems. They tell us what matters, what needs attention. Even brain science supports this: the amygdala, the brain's emotional center, reacts to feelings with intense energy. But when we acknowledge these feelings, the prefrontal cortex, the part responsible for reasoning helps us understand and manage them. This balance between feeling and thinking is the heart of emotional intelligence.

Imagine a river flowing freely. If blocked, it floods and causes destruction; if allowed to flow naturally, it nourishes the land. Our emotions are just like that river. So today, try this: when a difficult feeling arises, pause. Take a deep breath. Name it silently: "This is sadness," or "This is fear." Notice how it moves through your body, tightness in the chest, heaviness in the limbs, a flutter in the stomach. Don't push it away. Let it be.

This simple act of noticing without judgment begins healing. It shows your brain that the feeling is safe to express. Over time, this practice builds emotional strength, a quiet power that no storm can break. You don't have to be perfect at this. You don't have to have all the answers. You only need the courage to feel, one moment at a time. Because in the courage to feel, you find your true self which is unshaken, whole, and ready to shine. Have you ever noticed how the voice inside your head talks to you? Sometimes it cheers you on, but often it's critical, harsh, or doubtful. That voice, your inner dialogue shapes how you feel, how you see yourself, and how you respond to life's challenges.

Research shows that our brains are wired to respond to words whether spoken aloud or silently in our thoughts. When the inner voice is kind and encouraging, it activates areas in the brain linked to positive emotions, motivation, and resilience. But when it's negative and harsh, it triggers stress hormones like cortisol, making us feel anxious, sad, or defeated. Yet, most people treat their inner voice like a relentless judge, forgetting that this voice can also be their greatest friend. Changing that voice isn't about pretending everything is perfect or ignoring problems. It's about learning to speak to yourself as you would to someone you deeply care about — with patience, kindness, and understanding.

Imagine, If a close friend came to you feeling lost or scared, would you tell them they're worthless? Would you say, "You're hopeless," or "You'll never succeed"? Of course not. You would listen, comfort, and gently encourage.

So why do we say those things to ourselves? Self-compassion is the practice of treating yourself with the same kindness you offer others. It's been shown to reduce depression, increase happiness, and improve motivation. When you treat yourself with care, your brain's stress response lowers, and your ability to cope with difficulties improves. Begin with small steps. Notice your inner critic but don't believe everything it says. Instead, respond with kindness. For example, if your inner voice says, "You failed," reply gently, "I'm learning, and it's okay to make mistakes." This simple shift rewires your brain. It changes the conversation from a battle to a friendship. And over time, your inner voice will become a source of strength and encouraging you to keep going even when life feels heavy. Remember, you are the one who lives with yourself every moment. Make that relationship one of love, not judgment. We often think that big success comes from big, dramatic changes like starting a new job, moving cities, or having a sudden breakthrough. But the truth is far simpler, and far more within your reach. The real magic happens in the little things we do every day. Our habits those small, repeated actions are the invisible architecture of our lives.

Consider this: brushing your teeth, tying your shoes, or making your bed. These are habits you do without thinking, yet they keep you healthy, prepared, and organized. Now imagine if you applied that same simple power to your dreams and wellbeing. Research in neuroscience shows that habits are formed by the brain creating strong connections between actions and rewards. When you repeat something regularly, your brain starts to run it automatically, freeing up energy for other challenges. This means you don't need to rely on motivation alone because motivation can be fleeting. Instead, you build systems that make good actions effortless. For example, if you want to read more, start with just five minutes every day. Not one hour or ten pages just five quiet minutes. Over time, your brain will crave that peaceful moment, and five minutes will become fifteen, then thirty. Without pressure, without guilt. Habits create momentum, and momentum is a powerful force. Like a rolling stone gathering speed, each small step makes the next one easier. And before you know it, you're moving forward with a strength that feels natural and unstoppable. Habits aren't about perfection. There will be days when you miss your practice, or feel too tired. That's part of the journey. What matters is the choice to start again, not the rare slip. This is the quiet power of consistency. It outshines bursts of energy and fleeting inspiration. It's what transforms ordinary people into legends. So today, look at your daily life. What small habit can you start, just for five minutes? What simple act of care or growth can become your new rhythm? Small steps, done often, become your steady light, the light that never leaves. Resilience is often called the ability to bounce back from difficulties. But resilience is more than just recovering. It's growing stronger because of the challenges we face. It's a muscle we can train, like any other. Science shows that people who develop resilience have healthier brains and bodies. They experience less stress, recover faster from illness, and enjoy better mental health. Resilience doesn't mean we won't feel pain or sadness. It means we learn to move through those feelings without being overwhelmed.

But how do we build this strength? First, by accepting that life will have hardships. No one is immune. Accepting difficulty doesn't mean giving up. It means being realistic and preparing yourself to face storms with courage.

Second, by creating support systems. Humans are wired for connection. Friends, family, mentors, these relationships provide shelter when the rain falls. Studies show that strong social support is one of the best predictors of resilience.

Third, by practicing self-care. Resilience is easier to maintain when your body is rested, nourished, and cared for. Simple habits like good sleep, healthy food, and movement keep you physically ready to face challenges.

Fourth, by focusing on what you can control. Often, pain comes from worrying about things beyond our reach. Resilient people focus their energy on actions and thoughts they can influence, letting go of what they cannot.

Finally, by cultivating hope. Hope is a quiet, persistent belief that things can get better. It's not blind optimism but a grounded expectation born from past survival and inner strength.

Resilience is not about never falling. It's about how you rise again and again.

You are stronger than you think. Every hardship you've faced has built the foundation for your resilience. And this foundation will carry you forward, no matter what comes. Purpose is more than a goal or a job. It is the quiet fire burning inside, a reason to wake up every morning with hope and determination. Purpose gives life meaning, and meaning gives us strength when the world feels heavy. Many people spend years searching for purpose, thinking it must be a grand or complicated thing. But purpose often reveals itself in simple acts like caring for others, creating something beautiful, learning and growing. Science confirms that having purpose improves mental and physical health. People with a clear sense of purpose live longer, experience less depression, and recover faster from illness. Purpose helps the brain stay focused, motivated, and resilient.

Finding purpose begins with listening to yourself - your values, passions, and dreams. What makes your heart beat faster? What activities make time feel like it flies? What injustices or problems stir a deep feeling in you? Sometimes purpose is connected to serving others, sometimes it is about mastering a craft, or building a family, or creating art. There is no single path. The key is to find what deeply matters to you.

Once you identify your purpose, it acts like a compass, guiding your choices and giving your actions meaning. Challenges become lessons; failures become stepping stones; every day feels part of a larger story.

Purpose isn't fixed. it grows and changes as you do. It can be shaped by experiences, relationships, and inner reflection. So, take a moment today to ask yourself: what matters most to me? What small step can I take now that aligns with my deeper purpose? This quiet fire of purpose is your inner light. Nurture it, and it will never leave you. The voice inside your mind is powerful. It whispers stories about who you are, what you deserve, and how your day will go. This internal conversation shapes your world more than you might realize. When the voice is gentle and kind, you feel uplifted and ready to face life's challenges. But when it's harsh or critical, your heart feels heavy, and your confidence dims. But changing this inner voice is not about blind positivity or ignoring pain. It is about courage. The courage to face your feelings honestly, without judgment. When you allow yourself to feel sadness, anger, or fear, you give those feelings space to pass through instead of building walls inside you. This courage to feel is like opening a window in a stuffy room. Fresh air comes in, and the heaviness lifts. You begin to understand your emotions rather than being overwhelmed by them. Over time, this practice builds emotional strength. When you face your emotions with kindness, your inner critic loses power. Instead of berating yourself for feeling down or scared, you start speaking words of comfort and encouragement.

One way to practice is to talk to yourself as you would to a dear friend. If that friend is sad or struggling, you offer love and support, not harsh judgment. Try this now—when a negative thought arises, pause and ask, "What would I say to a friend feeling this way?" Then say those words to yourself.

This simple act may feel strange at first, but with patience, it becomes a natural habit. Your inner voice changes from a harsh judge to a compassionate guide. Remember, feeling vulnerable is not weakness. it's a sign of being human. Every person, no matter how strong they seem, has moments of doubt and fear. The key is to welcome those feelings instead of fighting them. The courage to feel deeply connects you to yourself. It makes your joy brighter, your sorrow lighter, and your life richer. Building kindness toward yourself is like planting a garden. At first, the soil may be hard and rocky, but with care and patience, life begins to grow. The first step is to notice the moments when your inner voice turns harsh. These moments are opportunities to pause and choose a different way. One powerful tool is mindfulness, the practice of paying gentle attention to your thoughts and feelings without judgment. Mindfulness teaches us to observe emotions as they come and go, like clouds drifting across the sky. When you practice this regularly, you stop getting caught up in painful stories or worries. Instead, you become an observer of your mind's activity.

Scientific studies show that mindfulness reduces anxiety and depression by calming the brain's fear centers. It strengthens areas responsible for emotional regulation and empathy. This means mindfulness not only makes you feel better but actually changes your brain's structure for the good. Try this simple exercise: when you feel a difficult emotion, stop and take three deep breaths. Focus on the rise and fall of your chest. Notice the feeling in your body without trying to push it away or hold onto it. You might feel tightness, warmth, or a flutter. Just observe and name it quietly in your mind — "sadness," "anger," or "fear." Naming emotions is a powerful act. It helps your brain make sense of what's happening and reduces their intensity. It's like turning on a light in a dark room—you suddenly see the edges clearly and can move with more ease. Over time, this practice builds emotional resilience. You learn that feelings come and go, and none of them lasts forever. This understanding helps you stay grounded when life feels overwhelming. Another important part of kindness is forgiving yourself. We all make mistakes, sometimes big ones. The inner critic loves to replay those moments and punish us again and again. But forgiveness means releasing that old pain. It doesn't mean forgetting or excusing mistakes, but allowing yourself to heal and grow. Ask yourself: "What can I learn from this? How can I be gentler with myself?" These questions open the door to compassion. When you forgive yourself, you create space for joy and peace to enter. Kindness toward yourself is not selfish. It is the foundation for loving others and living fully. When you nurture your own heart, you become stronger, calmer, and more joyful. The courage to feel deeply and kindly is a gift you give yourself every day. It is the light that never leaves, guiding you through darkness and into growth. Expressing emotions openly is one of the bravest acts we can do. It takes courage to show the world what we feel inside, especially when those feelings are vulnerable like sadness, fear, or anger. Yet, sharing emotions is a powerful way to connect with others and deepen our understanding of ourselves.

Humans are wired for connection. When we share honestly, our brains release oxytocin, often called the "bonding hormone." Oxytocin creates feelings of trust, safety, and love. It helps relationships grow stronger and makes us feel supported. But many of us learn early to hide our feelings. Maybe because society teaches that emotions are signs of weakness, or because past experiences taught us to protect ourselves. This silence can build walls, making us feel lonely, even when surrounded by others. Learning to express emotions takes practice. Start by naming your feelings not just to yourself, but sometimes to someone you trust. You don't need to have all the answers or fix the problem. Simply saying, "I feel hurt" or "I am scared" can relieve the weight inside. Research shows that bottling emotions can increase stress and even harm the immune system. On the other hand, expressing feelings even difficult ones promotes healing and well-being. In families and friendships, open emotional sharing creates a safe space where everyone feels seen and heard. It encourages empathy and compassion. When one person speaks their truth, it invites others to do the same. But expressing feelings doesn't mean letting emotions control you. It means being honest while staying grounded. This balance is a skill one that grows stronger with time. Try starting small. Write your feelings in a paper, or talk to a close one you want. Notice how it feels to let your emotions breathe instead of locking them away. With each expression, you break the chains of fear and isolation. You invite healing and growth, not just for yourself but for everyone around you.

The courage to feel is not just about survival. It is about living fully, deeply, and with heart. When we embrace our emotions instead of hiding them, something magical happens and creativity begins to flow. Emotional courage doesn't just help us survive life's challenges; it opens the door to innovation, new ideas, and fresh ways of thinking. Studies show that people who are emotionally aware are often more creative. This happens because emotions fuel imagination. When you allow yourself to feel deeply joy, sadness, frustration and by the way you also unlock new perspectives. These feelings inspire art, music, writing, and problem-solving. Think about some of the greatest inventions or works of art in history. Many were born from a place of intense emotion which associated with pain, hope, love, or anger. Emotions push us to explore new territories, to express what words alone cannot capture.

Creativity isn't only for artists or inventors. Every one of us can tap into this creative energy. When you courageously explore your feelings, you learn more about what moves you. This insight helps you find unique solutions to everyday problems whether at work, in relationships, or personal growth.

Another surprising fact from neuroscience: emotional openness improves brain connectivity. The more you allow yourself to feel and express emotions, the more your brain areas communicate. This improves thinking, memory, and decision-making skills essential for success in all areas of life. Allowing emotions to flow also nurtures intuition, your inner guidance system. When you listen to your feelings without judgment, you become more attuned to subtle signals from your mind and body. Intuition often leads to breakthroughs that logic alone cannot provide. Sometimes, fear or shame holds us back from expressing emotions fully. But taking small steps to share your feelings can rewire your brain for greater freedom and creativity. Over time, emotional courage becomes a habit that fuels innovation. Imagine a life where your feelings don't block your path but light the way. Where your deepest emotions become sources of strength and inspiration. This is the power of the courage to feel. It's not just about understanding emotions but using them to create a richer, more vibrant life. Cultivating emotional courage every day begins with small, intentional steps. Like any skill, it grows stronger the more you practice. The first step is simply to notice your feelings—not to change or judge them, but to accept their presence.

Start your day by checking in with yourself. Ask quietly, "How do I feel right now?" You might be surprised how often this simple question is overlooked. Awareness is the foundation of courage. It helps you catch feelings before they grow into overwhelming storms. When difficult emotions arise, don't push them away. Instead, try to meet them with curiosity. What is this feeling trying to tell me? Where do I feel it in my body? Naming and exploring emotions helps dissolve fear and confusion.

Another practical tool is journaling. Writing down your thoughts and feelings gives them a safe space to be expressed. You don't need to write perfect sentences, just let your words flow. This act can be deeply healing, providing clarity and release. Remember, emotional courage also means setting healthy boundaries. Sometimes, protecting your heart means saying no to people or situations that drain your energy. Boundaries are not walls; they are bridges to self-respect and balance. Daily mindfulness practices support emotional strength. Spend a few minutes each day simply breathing and observing your thoughts. This creates a calm space inside you, a place where feelings can come and go without chaos. It is also important to reach out for support when needed. Sharing your feelings with trusted friends or mentors builds connection and reminds you that you are not alone. Vulnerability shared becomes strength multiplied. Every step toward emotional courage deepens your relationship with yourself. It builds resilience against life's storms and opens the door to genuine happiness. Remember, the courage to feel is a lifelong journey, not a destination. It asks for patience, kindness, and above all, love for yourself. This journey will carry you through every chapter of your life, making each moment richer and more meaningful. What we often don't realize is how deeply our emotions affect our physical health. The courage to feel isn't only about mental strength. It also plays a crucial role in our body's well-being.

Scientists have found that unexpressed emotions can create stress that weighs heavily on the body. When feelings like anger, sadness, or anxiety are bottled up, they trigger the release of stress hormones like cortisol. Over time, this constant flood of stress chemicals can damage the heart, weaken the immune system, and even cause chronic pain. On the other hand, allowing yourself to experience and express emotions can lower these harmful stress levels. People who openly acknowledge their feelings often have lower blood pressure, better sleep, and stronger immune responses. It's like emotional honesty acts as a natural medicine for the body. Think about times when you've felt deeply sad or scared but allowed yourself to cry or talk about it. Afterward, there is often a sense of relief, a lightness that comes from releasing pent-up feelings. This release helps the nervous system reset and brings balance back to the body. Even laughter, a joyful expression of emotion, has incredible health benefits. It reduces stress hormones, boosts immune cells, and triggers the release of endorphins, the body's natural painkillers. Emotional courage to express happiness is just as important as allowing sorrow or anger. Our bodies and minds are connected in ways we're only beginning to understand. When we practice emotional courage, we create harmony between these two parts of ourselves. This harmony is essential for true wellness. Taking care of emotional health through courage and honesty is not a luxury. It is a vital part of living a full, vibrant life. By accepting your feelings fully, you build a foundation of strength that supports every breath, every heartbeat, every step you take. Our earliest experiences shape how we understand and express emotions. Childhood is the foundation where the courage to feel either grows strong or becomes fragile. The way caregivers respond to our feelings teaches us if it's safe to express joy, sadness, anger, or fear.

If a child's emotions are accepted and met with kindness, they learn that feelings are natural and okay. This early acceptance builds a strong emotional foundation. The child grows into an adult who trusts their feelings and can face life's ups and downs with resilience. But when feelings are dismissed, ignored, or punished, the opposite happens. The child may learn to hide emotions to avoid rejection or pain. Over time, this creates walls that block feelings, making it harder to be vulnerable or open later in life. Healing from childhood emotional wounds is part of the journey toward courage. It means gently uncovering old fears and doubts and choosing to respond differently now. Therapy, self-reflection, or supportive relationships can help in this process. An important truth is that it's never too late to learn emotional courage. We can rewire old patterns by practicing kindness toward ourselves and others. Each small step toward feeling deeply and honestly rewrites the story written long ago. Remember, the past does not have to define your present or future. Emotional courage gives you the power to heal, grow, and create new, healthier connections with yourself and the world. The bravery to face these old wounds, to feel what was once too painful, is itself a beautiful act of strength. Relationships whether with family, friends, or partners thrive on emotional courage. When we show up honestly with our feelings, we build trust, understanding, and deep connection. Without this courage, relationships can become distant or filled with misunderstandings.

Imagine a friendship where both people can openly share joy and pain, hopes and fears. This openness creates a safe space where both feel valued and accepted. Emotional courage allows us to say, "I'm hurt," or "I need help," without fear of judgment or rejection. This kind of vulnerability strengthens bonds. It teaches us empathy, the ability to truly understand and feel what another person is going through. Empathy, in turn, nurtures kindness and patience. When emotional courage is missing, small problems grow into big conflicts. Feelings get buried, resentments build, and communication breaks down. Many relationships suffer not because people don't care, but because they are afraid to be fully seen. In romantic relationships, emotional courage is especially vital. It helps partners navigate challenges with honesty and respect, rather than avoidance or blame. Sharing feelings can be difficult, but it lays the foundation for true intimacy. Families too benefit when members practice emotional courage. Children learn how to express themselves by watching the adults around them. When parents and caregivers model honesty and acceptance, children grow up with healthy emotional tools.

Practicing emotional courage in relationships is a gift not just to others, but to ourselves. It frees us from loneliness and invites love and support into our lives. The courage to feel deeply and share openly connects hearts and builds bridges that last a lifetime. Fear and uncertainty are among life's most common challenges. Yet, many of us try to avoid feeling these emotions, thinking they are signs of weakness. But emotional courage teaches us something different. It shows us that facing fear is a form of strength. When we accept fear instead of running from it, we begin to understand its message. Fear is often a signal that we are stepping into new territory, growing beyond our comfort zone. Without fear, there is little change or progress.

Accepting uncertainty means living with open hands, ready to accept whatever comes next. This is not easy. Our brains are wired to seek safety and predictability. But life itself is unpredictable, and emotional courage helps us dance with that uncertainty instead of resisting it. Research shows that people who face fear with openness experience less anxiety in the long run. By allowing fear to be present, we reduce its power over us. This creates space for clarity and calm, even in difficult situations. It is helpful to remember that courage doesn't mean the absence of fear. It means acting in spite of fear. Each time you choose to feel fear fully and keep moving forward, you build inner strength that lasts. Over time, emotional courage transforms fear from a barrier into a guide. It helps us discover hidden resources within ourselves - resilience, creativity, and hope. So next time fear knocks at your door, invite it in. Listen carefully, and then choose how you will respond. This is the path to true freedom. Emotional courage and self-compassion walk hand in hand. To face our feelings bravely, we must also be gentle with ourselves. Self-compassion means treating yourself with the same kindness you would offer a dear friend who is hurting. Often, when emotions are difficult, we become our own harshest critics. We say things like, "I shouldn't feel this way," or "I'm weak for being upset." These thoughts only deepen pain and build walls around our hearts.

But true courage asks for softness too. It invites us to sit quietly with our feelings, without judgment or blame. Imagine wrapping yourself in a warm blanket of kindness when the world feels cold and overwhelming. Research reveals that self-compassion reduces anxiety and depression. It strengthens resilience and improves overall well-being. When you respond to your struggles with care instead of criticism, you create a safe place inside, a home for healing. Self-compassion also encourages growth. When mistakes happen, it says, "It's okay to be imperfect. You are learning." This mindset opens the door to forgiveness and new beginnings. Learning emotional courage is not about being tough all the time. It's about being brave enough to be gentle especially with yourself. Each act of kindness toward your own heart builds a stronger foundation to face life's storms. Nurturing self-compassion starts with small, everyday habits that remind us to treat ourselves with kindness. One simple practice is to notice your inner dialogue. What do you say to yourself when things get tough? If your thoughts are harsh, try gently shifting them to more supportive words. For example, instead of thinking, "I always mess up," say, "I'm doing my best, and it's okay to make mistakes." This simple change can lighten the weight on your heart and open space for growth.

Another helpful habit is taking moments throughout the day to pause and breathe deeply. These small breaks create calmness inside, allowing you to reconnect with yourself and your feelings without overwhelm. Writing a few kind sentences about yourself each morning or night can also build self-compassion. You might write, "I am worthy of love," or "I am learning to be gentle with myself." These affirmations, repeated over time, become powerful reminders of your own value. Physical self-care is a part of self-compassion too. Nourishing your body with good food, rest, and movement shows respect for yourself. When your body feels cared for, your heart feels safer to open and heal. Remember that everyone struggles sometimes. You are not alone in your feelings or challenges. Connecting with others who practice kindness toward themselves can inspire and encourage your own journey. Building self-compassion is like planting seeds. With patience and care, these seeds grow into a garden of strength, peace, and courage. Emotional courage shapes the way we make decisions and grow as individuals. When we face our feelings honestly, we gain clarity about what truly matters to us. This clarity guides us to make choices aligned with our values and dreams. Without emotional courage, decisions are often clouded by fear, doubt, or the desire to please others. We might choose comfort over growth, or avoidance over change. These choices may feel safe at the moment but leave us feeling stuck or unfulfilled.

When we allow ourselves to feel fully whether joy, sadness, excitement, or fear, we tap into deeper wisdom. Our emotions carry important information about our needs and desires. Listening to this inner voice helps us move forward with confidence.

Research in psychology shows that people who are emotionally aware and courageous tend to have greater life satisfaction and resilience. They face challenges with an open heart and learn from every experience, good or bad. Growth comes from stepping into discomfort with courage. It means being willing to try new things, risk failure, and embrace uncertainty. Emotional courage gives us the strength to face these moments and keep moving. Personal growth is a journey, not a destination. Every decision made with emotional honesty is a step toward becoming the fullest version of yourself. As you practice emotional courage, you'll find your decisions becoming clearer, your path brighter, and your spirit stronger. Failure is often seen as something to fear or avoid. But emotional courage teaches us to view failure differently — not as a defeat, but as a powerful teacher. When we face failure with open hearts, we unlock valuable lessons that shape our future. The fear of failing holds many people back. It whispers, "What if you're not good enough?" or "What if things never get better?" These thoughts can stop us from trying, dreaming, or growing. Yet, the truth is that failure is a natural part of every journey worth taking. When we feel our disappointment or frustration fully, without shutting it down, we begin to understand what went wrong. This honest feeling helps us learn not just intellectually, but deeply in our hearts. It builds resilience and prepares us to try again with new insight.

History is full of stories where failure was the stepping stone to success. But behind every story is someone who had the courage to feel the pain of failure, heal, and keep moving forward. Failure does not define your worth. It only shows that you are brave enough to step out of your comfort zone. The courage to feel the sting of failure is what makes success truly meaningful.

Every failure is a gift in disguise, wrapped in lessons that guide us toward wisdom, strength, and deeper courage. Resilience is the ability to bounce back from difficulties, to keep going even when life feels heavy. Emotional courage is the key that unlocks resilience. When we allow ourselves to feel deeply, even pain or sadness, we build the strength to rise again. It may seem strange that feeling vulnerable can make us stronger. But every time we face our emotions honestly, we practice resilience. Like a muscle that grows with exercise, our inner strength expands when we meet challenges head-on. Studies show that people who practice emotional courage have better mental health and cope more effectively with stress. They don't avoid hard feelings; instead, they acknowledge them and move through them with kindness and patience. Building resilience doesn't mean never feeling weak or tired. It means accepting those moments without judgment and trusting that they will pass. This trust in yourself is a powerful form of courage.

You can nurture resilience by taking small steps every day. Pausing to breathe during stress, reaching out for support, or simply reminding yourself that this moment will pass. Each act of courage strengthens the roots of your spirit, helping you weather life's storms with grace and hope. Emotional courage not only helps us face pain but also opens the door to gratitude and joy. When we allow ourselves to feel fully, we become more aware of the little blessings often hidden in everyday life. Gratitude is a powerful emotion that shifts our focus from what is lacking to what is present and good. It helps us see beauty even in difficult times. But to feel gratitude deeply, we must first be willing to experience our full range of emotions honestly. It takes courage to recognize joy without guilt or fear that it might disappear. It takes courage to be thankful even when life is challenging. This courage transforms gratitude into a steady light that warms our hearts. Scientific studies confirm that practicing gratitude regularly improves mental and physical health. It reduces stress, improves sleep, and builds stronger relationships. Emotional courage encourages us to embrace gratitude as a natural part of healing and growth. Joy and gratitude often live side by side with sorrow and struggle. They are not opposites but companions on life's journey. Emotional courage helps us hold both gently, creating a richer, fuller experience of life. By choosing to notice and appreciate even small moments of joy, we build a foundation of happiness that supports us through harder days. Emotional courage strengthens not only our relationship with ourselves but also deepens our connection with others. When we bravely share our true feelings, we invite others to do the same, building trust and understanding.

Many people hide their emotions out of fear. Fear of judgment, rejection, or being misunderstood. But holding back feelings creates distance, like a wall between hearts. Emotional courage helps us tear down these walls. Being honest about our emotions can feel scary. It requires vulnerability, which some might confuse with weakness. But real strength lies in showing up as we are, imperfections and all.

When we practice this kind of openness, we nurture empathy. Others can see our humanity and relate to our struggles. This shared vulnerability creates bonds that comfort and uplift us. Science shows that close, honest relationships improve our well-being and lengthen our lives. Emotional courage is the key to forming these authentic connections. By letting others see the real you, you create a space where love and support flow freely. This is the true gift of courage. The power to connect deeply, heal together, and grow stronger as one. Setting healthy boundaries is an act of emotional courage that protects our well-being and nurtures respect in relationships. Boundaries help us define what feels safe and comfortable, allowing us to care for ourselves without guilt or fear. Many people struggle with saying no or expressing their needs clearly. They worry about disappointing others or causing conflict. But true courage lies in standing up for yourself kindly and honestly. When we set boundaries, we teach others how to treat us. Boundaries create a safe space where both people can be themselves without fear or resentment. They build trust and strengthen bonds. Emotional courage means recognizing your limits and honoring them, even when it feels uncomfortable. It's not selfish, it's necessary for balance and health. Research shows that people who maintain healthy boundaries experience less stress and greater happiness. They also develop stronger, more respectful relationships. Learning to say no or ask for what you need can be difficult at first. But with practice, it becomes easier and deeply empowering.

Boundaries are a form of self-respect and love. They protect your heart so you can give to others from a place of fullness, not emptiness. Forgiveness is one of the hardest acts of emotional courage we can practice, yet it is also one of the most freeing. Holding on to anger, resentment, or pain ties us to the past and keeps our hearts heavy. Forgiving doesn't mean forgetting or excusing harm. It means choosing to let go so we can heal. Emotional courage allows us to face the hurt honestly, feel the pain deeply, and then decide to release it. This is not a quick or easy process. It takes time, patience, and kindness toward ourselves. When we forgive, we free ourselves from the prison of bitterness. Studies show that forgiveness improves mental health, lowers stress, and even benefits our physical well-being. It opens space for peace and joy to grow. Forgiveness also means recognizing our own imperfections. Just as we need forgiveness from others, we must forgive ourselves for mistakes and regrets. Self-forgiveness is the foundation of emotional freedom. By choosing forgiveness, we reclaim our power. We no longer let the past control our present. Instead, we create room for love, hope, and new beginnings. This courageous act transforms wounds into wisdom and pain into strength. Forgiveness is not weakness—it is the bravest form of love. Emotional courage is the light that guides us toward a hopeful future. When we learn to face our feelings honestly and bravely, we unlock the power to create meaningful change in our lives. The future may be uncertain, but courage helps us move forward with faith rather than fear. It gives us the strength to dream big, to set goals, and to believe in our ability to grow.

Hope is not blind optimism. It is a quiet confidence born from facing life's challenges and choosing to rise again. Emotional courage fuels this hope by reminding us that even in darkness, there is a path to light. Every feeling you have is a gift — a signal from your soul guiding you toward growth and healing. Embrace your emotions with kindness and bravery, and the future will open before you like a sunrise. With courage in your heart, you are ready to walk forward, creating a life full of meaning, connection, and joy. Emotional courage is more than just facing difficult feelings. It is the steady light that leads us into a future full of hope and possibility. When we learn to meet our emotions honestly, without running away or suppressing them, we open a door to personal growth that no fear can close.

Life is always uncertain. We cannot predict exactly what tomorrow will bring. This uncertainty often causes anxiety and doubt. But emotional courage allows us to move forward anyway. It reminds us that while we cannot control everything, we can control how we respond. This choice, how we respond is where our real power lies. When you cultivate emotional courage, you start to see challenges not as threats but as opportunities to learn and grow. You develop a deep faith in your inner strength. This faith is not blind optimism or wishful thinking; it is built from experience, experiences where you felt pain, sadness, fear, and yet you chose to keep going. Each time you rise after falling, your hope grows stronger. Hope is like a seed planted deep inside your heart. It needs courage to grow, because the world will sometimes try to bury it under fear and doubt. But with every brave act whether it is asking for help, setting a boundary, forgiving someone, or simply choosing to feel your feelings, you water that seed. Eventually, it blossoms into a confident belief that life can be meaningful and joyful, no matter the obstacles. Emotions are messengers, not enemies. When you listen to your feelings with kindness, you learn important truths about yourself and your needs. Emotional courage means trusting these messages and letting them guide you toward healing and change. It means knowing that your feelings are not weaknesses but signals showing you the way forward. It walks beside you when the path is rough and when the skies are bright. It helps you trust yourself when others may not understand. It is the quiet voice inside that says, "You can do this," even when everything else shouts, "Give up." With emotional courage in your heart, you are not alone. You carry a light that will never go out, a light that will lead you to connection, to purpose, and to joy. The future is not something to fear but a canvas waiting for your brave brushstrokes. So, step forward with confidence. Embrace your full self, your whole story. The courage you have cultivated in this chapter is the foundation for all the growth and happiness still to come. Trust that as long as you keep feeling, learning, and moving forward, you are creating a life rich with meaning and love. Emotional courage is the quiet but powerful light that guides us toward a future filled with hope, meaning, and growth. It is the ability to face our feelings without running away, to welcome joy and pain alike, and to use these emotions as stepping stones rather than stumbling blocks. When we cultivate this courage, we unlock a deep well of strength that transforms uncertainty into opportunity.

Life's unpredictability is a source of fear for many. We worry about what tomorrow might bring but the unknowns that lurk just beyond our control. The emotional courage teaches us that while we cannot predict or control everything, we can control our response to life's challenges. This shift in perspective is profound. It puts us back in the driver's seat of our own journey. Research in psychology shows that people with high emotional resilience those who face emotions head-on tend to have better mental health, stronger relationships, and even longer lifespans. This resilience is rooted in courage: the courage to feel fully and honestly, to accept what is, and to keep moving forward. The act of embracing our emotions creates new neural pathways in the brain, making us mentally stronger over time.

Hope is a vital companion on this path. It is not blind optimism or wishful thinking. Rather, hope is a confident belief born from experience, experience where we endured hardship, felt pain, yet continued to believe in better days ahead. This belief fuels motivation and energizes our actions, even when the road is steep.Science supports this deeply human truth. Studies in neuroscience reveal that acknowledging and expressing emotions lowers stress hormones like cortisol, boosts immune function, and improves overall well-being. This means emotional courage is not just a poetic ideal. It is a biological necessity for a healthy, joyful life. The future is not something to fear but a blank canvas awaiting your brave brushstrokes. Each day, each moment, you have the power to choose courage over fear, hope over despair. This choice shapes not only your own life but also touches those around you in profound ways.

3. The Power of Mindset

The way we think shapes the way we live. Our mindset is the collection of beliefs and attitudes we hold about ourselves and the world acts like a lens through which we see everything. It colors how we interpret events, how we respond to challenges, and even how much joy or stress we feel in daily life. Scientists have discovered that mindset is not fixed. It can change, grow, and develop like a muscle, through practice and awareness. This means we are not prisoners of our past thoughts or habits. Instead, we have the power to rewire our minds and create healthier, happier ways of thinking. There are two main types of mindset that researchers often talk about: fixed mindset and growth mindset. A fixed mindset believes that our abilities and intelligence are static, something we are born with and cannot change. People with this mindset may avoid challenges, fear failure, or give up easily because they think their talents are limited. On the other hand, it sees challenges as opportunities to learn and improve. It understands that effort, learning, and perseverance can help anyone grow their skills and intelligence. This mindset embraces failures as lessons, not final judgments. It encourages curiosity and resilience. The power of mindset goes beyond just school or work performance. It deeply influences our emotional health, relationships, and even physical wellness. People with a this mindset tend to have lower stress, better problem-solving skills, and stronger connections with others. Research from renowned psychologist Carol Dweck and many others shows that shifting from a fixed to a growth mindset can literally change the way our brain works. When we believe we can improve, our brain creates new neural connections that support learning and creativity. This process is called neuroplasticity. Imagine your mind as a garden. With a fixed mindset, the garden is overrun with weeds negative thoughts like "I can't do this" or "I'm not good enough." But with a growth mindset, you become a gardener who plants seeds of hope, perseverance, and positivity. Over time, the garden blooms with confidence and joy.

The good news is that anyone can develop a growth mindset. It starts with awareness: noticing your inner thoughts and gently challenging those that limit you. It grows with practice: trying new things, embracing mistakes, and celebrating small victories. As we begin this chapter, remember: your mind is powerful, and your beliefs shape your reality. By developing a mindset of growth and possibility, you open the door to a richer, fuller life. The journey to change your mindset is itself a courageous act, one that will pay off in countless ways.

Now that we understand how powerful our mindset is, the next step is to learn how to recognize the thoughts and beliefs that hold us back. These limiting beliefs often hide quietly in the background, shaping our actions without us even realizing it. But once we bring them into the light, we can start to change them. Limiting beliefs often sound like "I'm not good enough," "I'll never succeed," or "It's too late for me." These ideas can feel so true that we accept them without question. Yet, they are just thoughts not facts. Many times, these beliefs are formed early in life, influenced by past experiences, disappointments, or even what others have told us.

The first practical step to shifting your mindset is awareness. Begin by paying attention to your inner dialogue. What do you say to yourself when you face a challenge? Do you encourage yourself or criticize? Awareness is not about judging your thoughts but simply noticing them, like a curious observer.

Next, question those limiting beliefs. Ask yourself: "Is this really true? What evidence do I have? Could there be another way to see this situation?" This simple questioning creates space between you and the belief. It weakens its hold and allows room for new, more positive ideas to grow.

One powerful technique is to replace limiting thoughts with positive affirmations that feel genuine. For example, instead of saying, "I can't do this," try, "I am learning and growing every day." These affirmations may feel strange at first, but with practice, they begin to rewire your brain toward optimism and possibility. Science supports this process. Studies on this show that repeated positive thoughts strengthen neural pathways linked to confidence and motivation. Just like exercise builds muscle, practicing positive thinking builds mental resilience.

Another key step is accept failure as part of the learning process. Many people avoid trying new things because they fear failure. But a growth mindset teaches us that mistakes are not setbacks but stepping stones to success. Each failure provides valuable feedback that helps us improve. Think of famous inventors like Thomas Edison, who said, "I have not failed. I've just found 10,000 ways that won't work." His success came from persistence and a mindset that saw failure as a natural part of discovery. To support your mindset shift, surround yourself with positive influences. People who believe in growth and encourage you. Limit time with those who reinforce negative thinking. The energy we absorb from others deeply impacts our own beliefs. Remember, changing mindset is not a one-time event but a lifelong journey. It takes patience, kindness, and commitment. Some days will be easier than others, but every small step forward adds up to big changes over time. As you continue, celebrate your progress. Each moment you choose growth over doubt, you strengthen your mind and heart. The power to shape your reality lies within you, starting with the thoughts you choose to nurture. Our mindset does not only live in our thoughts. It shapes every small choice we make throughout the day. These choices, repeated over time, become our habits, which in turn build the life we live. Understanding this connection between mindset and habits is a key to unlocking lasting change.

Imagine two people faced with the same challenge: learning a new skill, like a language or a musical instrument. One believes they are not naturally talented and feels discouraged at the first mistake. The other believes that with effort and patience, improvement is possible. Over time, the second person's mindset encourages daily practice, while the first gives up early. This difference in mindset leads to very different outcomes. Psychologists call this the "self-fulfilling prophecy." When we believe something will happen, our actions align to make it true. A fixed mindset can trap us in fear and self-doubt, limiting our potential. Habits are like the building blocks of our daily life. Tiny decisions, such as whether to get up early or stay in bed, to speak kindly or criticize, to take a deep breath or get overwhelmed, shape the bigger picture. When we nurture a growth mindset, we begin to build habits that support learning, kindness, and resilience. Science tells us that habits form in the brain through repeated behavior that creates strong neural pathways. The more we practice positive habits, the easier they become almost automatic. This is why small changes matter so much. A single moment of choice can be the seed of a new habit that changes everything. Each success builds confidence, which reinforces the belief that growth is possible. Another important habit is self-compassion. Many people push themselves hard but forget to be kind inwardly. When we treat ourselves with patience and understanding, we reduce stress and encourage a positive mindset. This doesn't mean avoiding responsibility but gently supporting ourselves through challenges. The connection between mindset and habits also shows up in how we handle setbacks. They see the setback as a chance to learn, not a final failure. This approach builds resilience, a vital quality for long-term success and happiness.

Ask yourself: what habits today reflect your mindset? Are they helping you grow or holding you back? The power to change lies in noticing and choosing. Every day, every moment is an opportunity to build habits that align with the mindset you want. Remember, no one is perfect, and change takes time. But with a gentle, consistent focus on mindset and habits, you create a strong foundation for a fulfilling life. This chapter will continue to explore practical ways to build this foundation in the coming pages. Our mindset not only shapes how we think and act individually, but it also deeply influences the way we connect with others. The quality of our relationships whether with family, friends, or colleagues is often a reflection of the beliefs we hold inside ourselves. When we approach relationships with a fixed mindset, we may believe that people cannot change, that conflicts are permanent, or that misunderstandings are signs of failure. This can create walls between people, making it hard to forgive, listen, or grow together. The fixed mindset tends to judge and label others quickly, leading to frustration and distance. On the other hand, It recognizes that people grow at their own pace and that every relationship requires effort and learning. Challenges and disagreements become opportunities to understand more deeply, communicate better, and strengthen bonds.

Research shows that people who adopt a growth mindset in their relationships experience greater satisfaction and intimacy. They are more likely to admit mistakes, apologize sincerely, and seek solutions rather than blame. This creates a safe space where trust can flourish. The way we talk to ourselves about others also matters. If we hold assumptions like "This person will always hurt me" or "They don't care," it colors our interactions negatively. But by shifting our mindset to curiosity and wondering why someone acts a certain way, or what they might be feeling, we open the door to empathy and compassion. Empathy is a superpower of the heart. It allows us to step into someone else's shoes and see the world from their point of view. This ability strengthens relationships and reduces conflicts. And the beautiful thing is, empathy itself can be cultivated by training our mindset toward openness and kindness. Another important aspect of mindset in relationships is forgiveness. Holding onto anger or grudges can weigh heavily on the mind and heart. Forgiveness creates space for healing and new beginnings. We often underestimate how much our mindset influences the energy we bring into our relationships. Positive energy attracts positivity, while negative energy can push others away. When we choose to carry a mindset of hope, respect, and understanding, we naturally invite others to respond in kind. Think of your relationships as gardens. They need care, attention, and patience to grow. With a growth mindset, you become a gardener who nurtures trust, communication, and love. The harvest is a life rich with meaningful connections that uplift and sustain you. As you read on, notice the relationships around you. What mindset do you bring into them? How might a shift in perspective deepen your bonds and bring more joy? The power to transform your relationships lies in the mindset you choose every day. Life often throws challenges our way like unexpected stress, loss, or moments when everything feels overwhelming. How we respond to these pressures depends largely on our mindset. Emotional resilience, the ability to bounce back from difficulties, is not a fixed trait but a skill shaped by how we think and feel.

This shift in perspective changes the entire emotional experience. We stop feeling powerless and start feeling empowered. Scientific studies confirm this. People who see stress as a challenge rather than a danger tend to have lower levels of anxiety and better overall health. Their bodies react differently, with lower cortisol (the stress hormone) levels, and their minds remain clearer and more focused. Building emotional resilience begins with awareness. Recognizing when you are stressed or overwhelmed allows you to take steps before feelings spiral out of control. Mindfulness practices simple moments of focused breathing or paying attention to the present - help create this awareness. They anchor us in the here and now, reducing anxiety about the future or regrets about the past. Another key element is self-talk. When negative thoughts rush in like "I can't handle this," "This is too much", please try gently reminding yourself, "I've faced hard things before and grown," or "I can take one step at a time." These affirmations strengthen resilience by reinforcing belief in your ability to cope. Connection with others also plays a crucial role. Sharing your feelings with trusted friends or family reduces the burden of stress. Sometimes, resilience means accepting what we cannot change and focusing on what we can control. This doesn't mean giving up but recognizing our limits and conserving energy for what truly matters. This balance is a hallmark of emotional strength. It's important to remember that emotional resilience is not about avoiding pain or discomfort.

Rather, it's about growing through those experiences with kindness toward yourself. Each challenge faced with courage and compassion adds a layer of strength that will support you in future trials. In the coming pages, you'll discover how to build mental flexibility, stay grounded in difficult moments, and recover more quickly after setbacks. This journey with the book will prepare you to face life's ups and downs with a mindset that keeps your heart steady and your spirit hopeful. Building emotional resilience and a growth mindset doesn't happen by accident. It requires daily practice. The good news is, small habits can create a powerful ripple effect in how you think, feel, and respond to life's challenges.

One of the most effective habits is **starting your day with intention**. Before the noise of the world takes over, spend a few quiet moments setting a positive tone. This could be as simple as listing three things you're grateful for or reminding yourself of a personal strength. This practice grounds your mind and helps you carry a mindset of possibility and hope throughout the day.

Another key habit is **reflecting on challenges with curiosity instead of judgment**. When something difficult happens, pause and ask yourself: "What can I learn from this? How can this experience help me grow?" This gentle curiosity shifts your brain away from stress and toward problem-solving. It turns setbacks into stepping stones rather than roadblocks.

The practice of **mindful breathing** is also a powerful tool to calm the mind and body. Even just a minute of deep, slow breaths can reduce tension and clear mental clutter. When faced with stress, consciously slowing your breath signals your nervous system to relax. Over time, this simple habit can transform how you handle pressure.

Journaling is another way to connect with your mindset and emotions. Writing down your thoughts can clarify worries, reveal patterns, and bring insight. You don't need to write pages, a few sentences a day can help you track your growth and celebrate small victories. This habit strengthens self-awareness, a cornerstone of resilience. Building a support network is equally important. Make it a habit to **reach out to someone you trust regularly** may be a friend, family member, or mentor. Sharing your feelings and experiences creates connection and reminds you that you're not alone. Humans are wired for connection; leaning on others is a sign of strength, not weakness.

Physical activity also plays a role in mindset. Exercise releases endorphins, a natural mood lifters and improves brain function. You don't need intense workouts; a daily walk or gentle yoga can boost your mental clarity and emotional balance.

Practice self-compassion daily. Treat yourself with the kindness you would offer a close friend. When mistakes happen, remind yourself that imperfection is part of being human. Self-compassion nourishes a growth mindset by reducing fear of failure and encouraging persistence. These small habits, practiced consistently, build a mental foundation that helps you face life's challenges with courage and grace. As you develop them, you will notice a shift not just in how you handle stress but in how you see yourself and the world around you.

Remember, growth is a journey, not a destination. Each day offers a new chance to strengthen your mindset, deepen your resilience, and move closer to the life you want to live. Our mindset doesn't just influence how we handle emotions and relationships. it also shapes how we think creatively and solve problems. When life throws unexpected puzzles at us, the way we approach these challenges can either open doors or close them shut. A growth mindset fuels creativity by encouraging curiosity and experimentation. When we believe that our abilities can improve, we're more willing to take risks, try new ideas, and learn from failure. Instead of fearing mistakes, we see them as clues on the path to discovery.

This mindset supports flexible thinking, which means being able to see multiple solutions rather than getting stuck on one "right" answer. Creativity also thrives when we allow ourselves to be playful. Think about how children explore the world without judgment or fear of failure. They try different ways to build, draw, or solve problems simply for the joy of learning. Rekindling this childlike curiosity can help adults break free from rigid thinking patterns. Another factor is the environment we create for ourselves. Surrounding ourselves with diverse ideas, people, and experiences feeds our creativity. Exposure to new cultures, books, music, or conversations sparks fresh insights and broadens our perspective.

The mindset to cultivate here is one of openness not just to new ideas but also to constructive feedback. Feedback is a gift that helps us improve, yet many shy away from it because it feels uncomfortable. When we shift our mindset to see feedback as a tool for growth, we accelerate our learning and enhance our creativity.

Problem-solving also benefits from mindfulness and patience. When we rush to fix things quickly, we might miss important details or jump to conclusions. Slowing down and observing the problem calmly allows us to gather more information and think more clearly. Breaking a problem into smaller parts makes it less overwhelming. Tackling each piece one by one can reveal solutions that were hidden in complexity. This method builds confidence and keeps us motivated. It's important to remember that creativity and problem-solving aren't limited to artists or inventors, they are vital skills in everyday life. Whether figuring out how to balance work and family, managing finances, or planning a trip, a growth mindset helps us approach these tasks with optimism and resilience.

So, next time you face a problem, ask yourself: How can I look at this differently? What new idea might I explore? What can I learn if things don't go as planned? These questions encourage a mindset that sees challenges not as barriers but as opportunities to grow and create. I will explore practical exercises and stories that will help you unlock your creative potential and solve problems with confidence and joy. Now that we understand how a mindset can unlock creativity and improve problem-solving, let's explore practical exercises that you can start today to nurture these skills. These simple daily habits not only sharpen your mind but also make facing challenges more enjoyable and less stressful.

One of the easiest exercises to boost creativity is **"The What If" game**. Every day, take a few minutes to ask yourself, "What if?" questions about your routine or challenges. For example, "What if I tried a different route to work?" or "What if I approached this problem from a new angle?" This practice encourages your brain to think beyond usual patterns and open doors to fresh possibilities.

Another effective exercise is **brainstorming without judgment**. When faced with a problem, write down all ideas that come to mind, no matter how wild or unrealistic they may seem. Don't evaluate or dismiss anything at this stage. This frees your mind to generate many options and reduces fear of failure. Later, you can review and refine these ideas with more focus.

Mind mapping is a creative tool that helps organize thoughts visually. Start with the central problem or goal in the middle of a page, then branch out ideas, solutions, or related topics. Seeing connections in this way sparks new insights and helps break complex problems into manageable parts.

A key part of creativity is **taking breaks** and letting your mind wander. Studies show that stepping away from a difficult task can lead to sudden "aha" moments. Even a short walk or a change of scenery refreshes your brain and increases creative thinking. Practicing **gratitude** also plays an important role. When you regularly note what you appreciate, your brain shifts toward positive thinking, which fuels creativity. Gratitude helps reduce stress and opens your mind to new opportunities rather than obstacles. To improve problem-solving, try **breaking problems into smaller steps**. Instead of trying to fix everything at once, identify the first small action you can take. Achieving small wins builds momentum and makes large challenges feel less daunting.

Another useful habit is to **ask "Why?" multiple times** when you face an issue. This technique, called the "5 Whys," helps uncover the root cause instead of just treating surface symptoms. For example, if you feel overwhelmed, ask why repeatedly until you find the core reason. Once you know the real cause, solutions become clearer.

Finally, **accept failure as feedback** is essential. Each mistake or setback is a lesson wrapped in disguise. Reflect on what you learned and how it moves you closer to your goals. This mindset makes failure less frightening and more motivating. Remember, creativity and problem-solving are muscles that grow stronger with practice. Incorporate these exercises into your routine, and over time, you'll notice new confidence in facing challenges and more joy in discovering solutions. Real-life stories have a unique power. They show us that mindset is not just theory but a living, breathing force that shapes our lives. In every corner of the world, people face hardships, yet some rise above with resilience and creativity. Their stories teach us how mindset can transform struggles into triumphs. Take the story of a young woman named Asha, who grew up in a small village with limited resources. School was a challenge; books were scarce, and teachers were few. But Asha had a curious mind and a heart full of hope. Instead of seeing obstacles as barriers, she viewed them as puzzles to solve. She made flashcards from old newspapers, taught herself by listening to radio programs, and asked questions relentlessly. Her mindset was one of growth and determination.

Years later, Asha became a teacher herself, inspiring children in her village to dream beyond their circumstances. Her mindset not only changed her life but also lifted her entire community. What made the difference? A belief that learning and growth were always possible, even in difficult conditions.

Similarly, imagine Raj, a man who lost his job during an economic downturn. Instead of sinking into despair, Raj took this setback as a chance to explore his passions. He began learning digital skills online, despite no prior experience with computers. With patience and persistence, Raj built a small business from home, offering services to local companies. His story shows that a growth mindset can turn failure into opportunity. These stories may feel far away or extraordinary, but the truth is, everyone faces challenges. The difference lies in how we respond. Do we freeze in fear or take steps forward? Do we see problems as dead ends or as invitations to think differently?

Your own life holds similar stories, moments when you overcame difficulties, learned something new, or surprised yourself with resilience. Reflect on these times. They are evidence of the power of mindset already at work inside you. Mindset is like a garden. It needs care, attention, and nourishment. When watered with positive habits and protected from weeds of doubt and fear, it grows strong. And just as plants in a garden affect each other, our mindset influences those around us. When you cultivate a mindset of hope and growth, you inspire others without even trying. Now, consider your daily routine. What small actions can you take to nurture your mindset? How can your attitude toward challenges shift from resistance to curiosity? These questions are the seeds of change. As we move forward in this book, remember these stories and your own inner strength. They remind us that mindset is not fixed. It is something we build every day, step by step, thought by thought. Behind the inspiring stories of mindset lies a fascinating truth: our brains are wired to grow and change throughout life. The brain's power to reorganize itself by forming new connections. It means that no matter your age or past experiences, your mind can develop new skills, habits, and ways of thinking.

For a long time, people believed that the brain was fixed after childhood, but science has proven otherwise. Neuroplasticity shows us that every thought we think and every experience we have shapes our brain's structure. When we practice positive habits, challenge ourselves, or learn new things, our brain creates new neural pathways, making those skills stronger and easier to access.

This explains why mindset matters so much. When you believe you can grow, your brain responds by working harder to create new connections. When you doubt yourself or fear failure, your brain becomes less flexible, making it harder to learn and adapt. For example, research shows that when students adopt a growth mindset, their brain activity changes during learning tasks. They show more engagement and better problem-solving skills. This is because they are more willing to try, make mistakes, and learn from them.

Another important part of brain science is the role of **dopamine**, a chemical that motivates us to pursue rewards. When you achieve a small success or make progress, dopamine is released, making you feel good and encouraging you to keep going. This reward system supports growth mindset by reinforcing positive actions. Even setbacks and failures are essential for brain growth. When you face a challenge and persist, your brain strengthens the circuits involved in focus and self-control. Over time, this makes you more resilient and capable of handling difficulties. What does this mean for you? It means that mindset is not just an idea. It is a biological process. Every effort you make to think positively, learn something new, or face fears helps build a stronger, more flexible brain. This also explains why habits matter. Repeating positive thoughts and actions rewires your brain, turning new behaviors into natural responses. For instance, practicing gratitude or daily reflection strengthens the brain areas responsible for emotional balance and happiness.

The science of mindset offers hope and practical guidance: change is possible. Your brain is a living organ that grows with your choices and actions. You are not stuck with the thoughts or limitations you once had. So, when you feel stuck or overwhelmed, remember that your brain is ready to adapt and grow. You have the power to change your mindset and transform your life by simply choosing to practice habits that feed your growth.

Now we'll look at specific daily routines and mental exercises and help you build a mindset that supports success, joy. Now that we understand the incredible science behind how our brain changes and grows, let's explore practical ways to train your brain every day. These exercises are simple but powerful, designed to help you build habits that strengthen your mindset and boost your confidence.

Next, challenge your brain with **new learning**. Pick a subject or skill you've never tried befor like learning a new language, playing a musical instrument, or even cooking a new recipe. When you stretch your brain in new directions, you activate neuroplasticity and create fresh neural pathways. Don't worry about perfection; the joy is in trying and growing.

Visualization is another powerful tool. Spend a few minutes imagining yourself succeeding at a goal or handling a challenge with confidence. Picture the details vividly: the sights, sounds, and feelings of success. This mental rehearsal prepares your brain to perform better when you face real situations, boosting motivation and reducing anxiety. Physical exercise also plays a big role. Moving your body increases blood flow to the brain, releasing chemicals that support learning and memory. Even a short walk outside can spark creativity and clear your mind. So, make time to move daily, even if it's just a few minutes. Build a habit of **positive self-talk**. Notice your inner voice and gently replace negative thoughts with encouraging words. Instead of "I can't do this," say "I am learning and getting better." This simple shift changes how your brain reacts to challenges and helps reduce stress.

These practices may seem small, but they are like seeds planted in fertile soil. With regular care, they grow into a resilient, creative, and confident mindset. Remember, the journey to a powerful mindset isn't about perfection. It's about progress and persistence. Every small step you take today strengthens your brain for tomorrow's challenges. As you try these exercises, notice how your thoughts and feelings change. Celebrate your efforts, no matter how small. This positive feedback loop is the heart of mindset growth.

In the next page, we will explore the connection between mindset and emotional health, and how mastering emotions is key to lasting change. Our thoughts and mindset are closely linked to our emotions. In fact, understanding and managing our emotions is one of the most important steps to building a strong, positive mindset. Emotions act like a compass, guiding us through life's challenges and opportunities. When we learn to recognize and work with our feelings instead of being controlled by them, we unlock new power within ourselves. Emotions like fear, anger, sadness, or joy are natural signals from our brain. They help us react quickly to situations and motivate us to take action. But sometimes, these feelings can become overwhelming, clouding our judgment and stopping us from moving forward. This is where mindset plays a crucial role. People with a growth mindset understand that emotions are temporary and manageable. They don't let a bad feeling define them or stop their progress. Instead, they observe their emotions like a curious scientist—asking, "Why am I feeling this? What can I learn from it?"

Scientific research shows that practicing **emotional intelligence** — the ability to identify, understand, and manage emotions improves mental health and decision-making. It strengthens relationships and builds resilience. When you develop emotional intelligence, you are less likely to react impulsively and more likely to respond thoughtfully. One practical way to build emotional intelligence is to practice **emotional labeling**. This means naming your feelings when they arise. Instead of just feeling "bad" or "upset," try to be specific: "I feel anxious," "I feel frustrated," or "I feel hopeful." Naming emotions helps reduce their intensity and gives your brain a chance to think clearly.

Another tool is **self-compassion**. Often, we are harsh critics of ourselves when we make mistakes or face failures. But treating yourself with kindness and understanding is essential. Self-compassion reduces stress and encourages a growth mindset by reminding you that everyone struggles and grows.

It's also important to recognize that some emotions, even difficult ones like sadness or anger, have value. They can signal when something needs to change or when you need to set boundaries. The key is not to suppress emotions but to accept them and choose how to act. Breathing exercises, mindfulness, and journaling, which we discussed earlier, are excellent ways to calm the mind and regulate emotions. These practices create space between feeling and reaction, giving you control over your mindset. Think about a recent moment when strong emotions affected your choices. How might understanding those feelings better help you respond differently next time? This reflection is the start of emotional mastery.

We will explore stories and examples of people who transformed their lives by mastering emotions, turning setbacks into growth, and how you can apply these lessons in your daily life. Take the story of Arjun, a young man from a small village. Arjun dreamed of becoming a teacher, but after failing his exams twice, he felt crushed by disappointment and fear. For a while, he thought his dreams were over. But one day, he decided to see his failure not as a stop sign, but as a lesson. He started paying attention to how his feelings affected his actions. Instead of running away from sadness or frustration, he allowed himself to feel them and then chose to keep trying.

Arjun's mindset shifted slowly but surely. He began practicing small daily habits like reading a little each day, talking to his teachers about his difficulties, and reminding himself that every failure was a step closer to success. His emotions, once heavy chains, became signals that guided him on how to improve. After many months, Arjun passed his exams with flying colors and became the teacher he dreamed of.

What can we learn from Arjun's story? First, emotions do not have to be barriers. They can be guides. Second, mindset is built through small, consistent actions. It's not about sudden miracles but about patience and persistence.

Another inspiring example is Lata, a woman who faced the loss of a loved one. The grief she felt was overwhelming, and for months, she struggled to find peace. But gradually, she learned to honor her emotions by expressing them through writing and talking with close friends. This emotional honesty helped her heal and find new meaning in life. Lata's mindset became one of acceptance and hope rather than despair.

Both Arjun and Lata show us that emotional resilience, the ability to bounce back from setbacks is a skill we can develop. Science supports this too. Studies on resilience find that people who practice mindfulness, gratitude, and emotional awareness recover faster from stress and are happier overall. You might wonder, "How do I start building this resilience?" The key is awareness. Notice how you react to challenges. Do you push feelings away or face them with curiosity? Remember, feelings are not permanent states but waves that rise and fall.

These stories are not just tales but mirrors reflecting your own potential. Your struggles, your emotions, and your mindset journey are unique. Yet, the path to growth is universal. Acknowledge your feelings, learn from them, and keep moving forward. As you continue reading, hold onto the idea that your mind and heart can grow stronger with each step.

One well-studied technique is **mindfulness meditation**. This practice involves paying full attention to the present moment your breath, your body, or your surroundings without judgment. Studies from universities around the world confirm that just 10 to 15 minutes of mindfulness daily can reduce anxiety, improve focus, and increase emotional regulation. When you train your brain this way, you create a mental "pause button" that helps you choose thoughtful responses instead of automatic reactions. Another powerful tool is **gratitude practice**. Psychologists have found that people who regularly write down or reflect on things they are grateful for report higher levels of happiness and lower levels of depression. Gratitude shifts your mindset away from scarcity and negativity toward abundance and hope. Even on difficult days, finding small reasons to be thankful rewires your brain for positivity.

Cognitive reframing is a mental skill that lets you see problems from different angles. Instead of thinking, "This is too hard," you might tell yourself, "This is an opportunity to learn." Research in cognitive behavioral therapy (CBT) shows that reframing negative thoughts reduces stress and improves mood. You can practice this by catching negative thoughts and consciously replacing them with more positive, realistic ones. Physical activity is another key factor in emotional resilience. When you exercise, your brain releases endorphins and other chemicals that boost mood and reduce pain. Even gentle activities like walking or stretching can calm your nervous system and improve sleep, which is vital for emotional health. Social connection also strengthens resilience. Studies show that having supportive friends or family members reduces the impact of stress and improves mental health. Sharing your feelings and challenges with trusted people creates a sense of belonging and relief. All these methods connect because they help you take control of your inner world—the place where mindset and emotions meet. By practicing mindfulness, gratitude, reframing, physical movement, social support, and goal-setting, you build a toolkit for emotional resilience that lasts a lifetime. Remember, building resilience is a journey, not a destination. There will be ups and downs. But with patience and daily practice, you'll find your mind and heart growing stronger, ready to face whatever life brings. Our mindset not only shapes how we handle challenges but also colors the way we connect with others. The quality of our relationships with family, friends, and even strangers depends a great deal on how we understand and manage our emotions. When we learn to control our inner world, we naturally build healthier, stronger bonds outside.

Research in psychology shows that people with a positive and flexible mindset tend to have more satisfying relationships. Why? Because they communicate better, listen more deeply, and handle conflicts with calm instead of anger. Emotional intelligence is the ability to recognize your own feelings and those of others is key here. When you understand your emotions, you can express yourself clearly and avoid misunderstandings. Think about moments when you felt truly heard and understood. What made that experience different? Chances are, the other person was patient and open, not rushing to judge or fix things. Developing this kind of presence in your relationships starts with how you treat your own emotions. If you are kind and patient with yourself, you naturally extend that kindness to others.

One important skill is **active listening**. It means fully focusing on the other person's words and feelings without planning your response while they speak. This simple act builds trust and connection. When your mind is calm and centered, you can listen without distractions or defensiveness. Conflict is inevitable in any relationship, but mindset shapes how we face it. People with a fixed or negative mindset often see conflict as a threat or proof of failure. Those with a growth mindset see it as an opportunity to understand, grow, and find solutions. This attitude reduces stress and promotes cooperation. Science also tells us that expressing gratitude and appreciation in relationships strengthens bonds. Small acts like saying "thank you," acknowledging someone's effort, or showing empathy activate positive emotions in both people, creating a cycle of goodwill.

Empathy itself is a powerful skill rooted in emotional awareness. It allows you to step into someone else's shoes and feel what they feel. This deep understanding often heals wounds faster than words. As you reflect on your relationships, notice how your mindset influences your responses. Are you quick to react or slow to judge? Are you open to understanding different viewpoints? Strengthening emotional intelligence and adopting a growth mindset can transform not just your inner life but your connections with others. Remember, mastering your emotions is not just about you — it is also about creating a ripple effect of kindness and understanding that touches everyone around you. Empathy and communication are the heartbeats of every meaningful relationship. They allow us to bridge gaps, heal wounds, and build trust. But like any skill, they require practice and patience. Empathy means truly understanding another person's feelings without judgment or distraction. Research in neuroscience shows that when we empathize, our brains actually mirror the emotions of others. This "mirror neuron" system helps us feel what others feel, making empathy a natural part of human connection. Yet, in today's busy world, distractions and stress often dull our ability to empathize. To sharpen empathy, the first step is to slow down. When someone shares their thoughts or struggles, give them your full attention. Listen not just to words but also to the feelings beneath. Notice their tone, pauses, and body language. This kind of listening creates a safe space where people feel valued. Communication is more than talking; it's about expressing clearly and listening deeply. According to psychologists, **nonviolent communication** which focuses on honest, compassionate dialogue builds stronger bonds than criticism or blame. Instead of saying, "You never listen to me," try, "I feel unheard when you look at your phone during our talks." This simple shift invites understanding rather than conflict. Another research-backed approach is using "I statements." These phrases own your feelings and needs without accusing others. For example, "I feel worried when plans change suddenly" opens dialogue without putting others on the defensive. This creates an atmosphere where problems can be solved together. Body language also speaks volumes. Maintaining eye contact, nodding gently, and keeping an open posture show that you care and are engaged. These small signals strengthen connection more than words alone.

Of course, communication isn't always easy. Emotions can get tangled, and misunderstandings happen. But practicing patience and humility helps. Remember, it's okay to pause, take a deep breath, and come back to the conversation when emotions settle. Writing down what you want to say before a tough talk helps clarify your thoughts and reduce stress. It also improves self-awareness, which feeds back into better communication. As you practice empathy and communication, you'll notice a positive change in your relationships. Conflicts will feel less threatening, and conversations will become opportunities for growth and connection. This ripple effect spreads beyond your close circle, touching workplaces, communities, and even strangers.

The power to transform your relationships lies in your mindset, the choice to listen with kindness and speak with honesty. This chapter will continue by exploring practical exercises to develop these skills further, helping you create bonds that nourish your heart and mind. Building empathy is like strengthening a muscle It grows stronger with regular exercise. Thankfully, these exercises are simple and can fit into everyday life. One of the most effective is called **perspective taking**. This means deliberately imagining the world from someone else's point of view.

Try this: Think about a recent disagreement or misunderstanding you had. Now, pause and ask yourself, "How might the other person have felt? What were they worried about or hoping for?" Doing this helps you move beyond your own reactions and opens the door to understanding. It softens judgments and builds compassion.

Another exercise is **empathic listening**. The next time someone shares something important with you, focus fully on their words. Avoid interrupting or preparing your response. Instead, after they finish, try repeating back what you heard, in your own words. For example, "So, you're saying you felt ignored when I didn't call?" This shows that you value their experience and encourages deeper connection. You can also practice **mindful empathy** through meditation. Sit quietly and think of someone you know who might be struggling. Silently wish them well, hoping for their happiness and peace. Studies have shown that this loving-kindness meditation increases feelings of empathy and reduces negative emotions. Journaling about your interactions with others is another powerful tool. Write about moments when you felt connected or disconnected. What emotions did you notice? How did your mindset affect the outcome? Reflecting like this sharpens your emotional awareness and helps you respond more thoughtfully in future encounters.

A fun but impactful practice is **reading fiction** or watching films that explore different lives and cultures. This kind of storytelling expands your empathy by immersing you in experiences very different from your own. Psychologists have found that people who regularly engage with stories tend to be more understanding and compassionate in real life. Remember, empathy is not about fixing others' problems or agreeing with everything they say. It's about acknowledging their feelings and experiences as real and important. When you do this, even difficult relationships soften, and healing begins. Don't forget self-empathy, being kind to yourself. When you understand and forgive your own mistakes, you build the foundation to do the same for others. Practicing self-compassion reduces stress and increases resilience, making empathy a natural part of your mindset. By regularly practicing these exercises, you strengthen the invisible threads that connect you with others. These threads create a network of support and understanding, enriching every relationship. In the next pages, we'll explore how to communicate assertively and kindly expressing your needs clearly without hurting others, a skill that perfectly complements empathy. **Assertive**

communication is a skill that balances honesty with respect. It allows you to express your thoughts, feelings, and needs clearly without being aggressive or passive. Many people struggle with this because they fear conflict or rejection, but the truth is that assertiveness builds trust and strengthens relationships.

At its core, assertive communication means standing up for yourself while also valuing others' feelings. Imagine a bridge connecting two people — assertiveness is the sturdy foundation that keeps that bridge strong and open. It prevents misunderstandings and resentment from building up silently over time. One practical method to communicate assertively is to use clear, direct language. Instead of beating around the bush or hoping others will guess what you want, say it plainly. For example, instead of saying, "It would be nice if you could help," try, "I need your help with this task by tomorrow." This clarity reduces confusion and shows you respect both your time and theirs. Another key to assertiveness is managing your tone and body language. Calm, steady voice and relaxed posture show confidence without aggression. Avoid yelling, sarcasm, or crossed arms, which can make others feel defensive. Instead, maintain eye contact and speak with a steady, warm tone.

Saying "no" can be one of the hardest parts of assertiveness. But it's important to understand that saying no doesn't mean you are selfish or unkind. It means you are honoring your limits. Practice polite but firm refusals like, "I appreciate the offer, but I can't commit right now." This shows respect for both yourself and the other person. Using "I" statements, as we discussed earlier, strengthens assertive communication. For example, "I feel overwhelmed when meetings run late" expresses your feelings without blaming others. This invites cooperation rather than conflict. Assertiveness also means asking for what you need without guilt. It's okay to request help, set boundaries, or share your opinions. When done kindly and clearly, people often respond positively because they know where you stand.

Remember, assertiveness is a skill learned over time. Start small maybe by speaking up in a meeting or expressing your preferences in daily situations. Notice how it feels to be honest and clear. Over time, this practice builds confidence and deepens your relationships. Scientific studies have shown that people who communicate assertively experience lower stress and higher self-esteem. Their relationships tend to be more satisfying because everyone's needs are respected and understood. Difficult conversations can feel scary or uncomfortable, but they are a part of life. How we handle these talks can change everything. When done well, even tough talks can bring people closer and solve problems. Science teaches us some simple ways to make hard conversations easier and more effective. First, it's important to stay calm. When emotions run high, our brain's "thinking part" – the prefrontal cortex – can get blocked by the "feeling part" – the amygdala. This makes it hard to listen or respond wisely. Taking deep breaths or pausing for a moment helps calm the amygdala and lets your thinking brain work again.

Next, try to listen carefully. This means really paying attention to what the other person is saying without planning your reply while they talk. Active listening shows respect and makes the other person feel heard. When someone feels understood, they are more open to finding solutions. It helps to use "I" statements, like "I feel worried when plans change suddenly," instead of blaming words like "You never tell me in time." This way, you share your feelings without making the other person defensive. Psychologists call this a way to lower "conflict heat." Choosing the right time and place for a tough talk is also key. Pick a quiet spot where you won't be rushed or interrupted. When both people feel safe and relaxed, conversations are more likely to be honest and kind.

Sometimes, it's okay to take breaks. If things get too heated, say something like, "I need a moment to think. Can we continue this later?" This pause helps both sides cool down and come back ready to talk calmly. Scientists have found that practicing these skills lowers stress hormones like cortisol. When stress is lower, we think clearer and communicate better. This improves relationships and even supports our health. Remember, the goal is not to "win" an argument but to understand and be understood. Difficult conversations are opportunities to grow trust, show care, and solve problems together. A positive mindset doesn't just happen by chance — it grows little by little through daily habits. When you practice positive thoughts and actions regularly, your brain builds stronger pathways that help you feel happier and more hopeful. One of the most powerful habits is gratitude. Taking time each day to notice and appreciate good things, even small ones, changes how your brain works. Studies show that people who practice gratitude have better sleep, lower stress, and stronger immune systems. It might be as simple as thinking, "I'm thankful for a sunny day" or "I appreciate my friend's kindness."

Another habit is mindfulness, paying close attention to the present moment without judgment. Mindfulness can be as easy as noticing your breath or the sounds around you. Research proves that mindfulness reduces anxiety and depression by calming the brain's stress centers. It helps you stay focused and react less to worries or negative thoughts. Exercise also plays a big role in mindset. When you move your body, your brain releases chemicals like endorphins and serotonin, which boost mood and energy. Even a short walk or stretching can clear your mind and improve how you feel. When you accomplish goals, your brain rewards you with a feeling of success. This encourages you to keep going, building confidence and strength in your mindset. As you practice gratitude, mindfulness, movement, goal-setting, and kind self-talk, your mindset will become your greatest ally in facing life's challenges. Fear is one of the most powerful emotions we experience. It is our brain's way of protecting us from danger. When we sense a threat, our body reacts quickly and the heart beats faster, muscles tighten, and adrenaline floods our system. This "fight or flight" response helped humans survive through history. But today, many fears come from our thoughts, not real dangers. One important fact is that fear is normal and natural. Everyone feels fear. What matters most is how we respond to it. If we let fear control us, it stops us from trying new things or chasing our dreams. But if we face fear with courage, it becomes less powerful.

A powerful way to face fear is through small steps. Psychologists call this "exposure." For example, if speaking in front of people scares you, start by talking in a small group, then slowly build up to bigger audiences. Each time you face fear, your brain learns that the danger isn't as big as it thought. Breathing techniques also help calm fear. Deep, slow breaths send signals to the brain that it is safe. This lowers heart rate and reduces feelings of panic. When fear comes, pause, breathe deeply, and remind yourself that you can handle this moment. Positive mindset plays a big role in overcoming fear. When you tell yourself, "I can do this," or "This feeling will pass," you train your brain to be stronger. Self-belief fuels courage. Courage is not the absence of fear. It is acting in spite of fear. Every brave act, no matter how small, builds your courage muscle. Fear — we all know it well. I have felt it many times, standing at a crossroads, unsure which path to take. Fear is natural; it has been with us since the beginning of time. Our ancestors needed it to survive. When danger was near, fear made their hearts race and bodies prepare to fight or run. But today, many fears come from inside our minds — from worries about what might happen, not what actually is happening.

From my own life, I've learned that fear is not the enemy. It's a signal, a message that something matters to us. But if we listen too closely and stop, fear grows bigger than it needs to be. It reacts fast, sometimes before we even realize it. That's why sometimes fear feels so overwhelming and automatic.

But here's what I have discovered through experience: fear doesn't have to control us. One step at a time, we can face it. When I was scared to speak in front of people, I started with just a few friends. It was uncomfortable at first, but each time I did it, the fear shrank a little. This is called "exposure," and research shows it helps our brain learn that the threat isn't as big as it thinks.

Another thing that helped me like when fear rushes in, I take slow, deep breaths. It's like telling my brain, "It's okay, we're safe." Science agrees that slow breathing calms the nervous system and slows the heartbeat. The most important lesson I've learned is that courage doesn't mean no fear. Courage means moving forward even when you're afraid. Each small step builds strength. Every time you face fear and don't run, you grow braver. Life is full of challenges. I've faced moments when everything seemed to fall apart — work pressure, personal doubts, or unexpected losses. In those times, resilience was what helped me stand up again. Resilience is not something we are born with; it is something we build, like a muscle, through experience and choice.

Scientists explain resilience as the brain's ability to adapt and recover from stress. When we face difficulties, resilient people don't just survive — they often grow stronger. But how do we develop this strength? From my own journey, I found that resilience starts with acceptance. Accepting reality doesn't mean giving up. It means seeing things clearly, without pretending problems don't exist. When I stopped fighting what was happening and instead asked, "What can I learn here?" I felt more in control. Another important part is having support. No one can be strong alone all the time. Friends, family, or mentors can give us the courage to keep going. Science backs this up, studies show people with strong social support handle stress better and recover faster.

I also learned that durability grows through small habits. Taking care of my body, getting enough sleep, eating well, and moving every day gave me energy and calm. Sometimes durability means changing how we think about failure. I used to fear failure deeply. But now I see it as a teacher, not a defeat. Each failure taught me something new about myself, my limits, or what to do differently next time. The truth is, life will test us. But resilience gives us the power to keep moving forward, to find light even in the darkest moments. Life's toughest moments don't come with warnings. From personal struggles to unexpected losses, these moments challenge us deeply. Through my own experiences, I realized that resilience is the secret power that allows us to bounce back when everything feels broken. But resilience is not some magic gift — it is a skill that anyone can develop.

Science calls resilience the brain's ability to adapt to stress and recover from setbacks. One surprising discovery is that durability grows when we accept reality as it is, not as we wish it to be. This acceptance is not about giving up; it's about seeing clearly without denial. Studies show that acceptance reduces anxiety and helps the brain conserve energy to find solutions instead of fighting invisible battles. In my own life, learning to say, "This is hard, but I can work through it," gave me a sense of calm and control.

Humans are social creatures, and support from others plays a huge role in resilience. Research from psychology confirms that people with strong social bonds recover faster from trauma and stress. During my difficult days, simply talking to a trusted friend or family member lifted a weight off my shoulders. The feeling of being understood and cared for is a powerful healing force.

Persistence also depends on physical health. The mind and body are deeply connected. Sleep, nutrition, and exercise influence how well we cope with stress. Scientific studies show that exercise releases brain chemicals like endorphins and BDNF (brain-derived neurotrophic factor), which help repair brain cells and improve mood. I noticed that even a short daily walk helped clear my mind and gave me energy to face problems with a fresh perspective. Lastly, reframing failure is a game-changer. Our brains are wired to avoid pain, so failure feels threatening. But research in positive psychology shows that seeing failure as feedback rather than defeat encourages learning and growth. Every time I faced setbacks, asking, "What did I learn?" helped me build courage and move forward.

Persistency is not about never falling; it's about rising stronger each time. The good news? With daily effort, anyone can cultivate this strength. As we move forward, I will share simple, science-backed habits that strengthen your mindset every day because the small things we do consistently shape the life we live.

4. Habits That Shape Your Life

Motivation is the hidden spark that keeps our habits burning. It doesn't stay strong all the time, some days it flares, and other days it barely glows. Learning how motivation works helps you stick with habits, even when you feel low on energy.

First, remember that habits give you structure. When you follow a routine like exercising every morning. You rely on the habit itself more than on your mood. Still, motivation makes habits shine, especially in the beginning. One powerful trick is to choose rewards that matter to you. Instead of waiting for a big prize, celebrate small wins: enjoy a moment of pride after ticking off your habit, or savor the calm you feel afterward. This little pat on your own back can feel even better than a fancy treat.

Visual feedback really helps, too. Marking each successful day on a calendar or in an app turns progress into something you can see. That steady string of checks reminds you, "I'm doing this," and urges you to keep going. And if you sense a loss of steam, have a simple backup plan ready: "If I can't run for thirty minutes today, I'll jog for five." Giving yourself a smaller step reduces the chance you'll quit altogether.

Willpower is often called our inner superhero but superheroes get tired. Each time you resist a temptation, a bit of your self-control is used up. That's why it's smarter to shape your surroundings so you don't have to fight temptation all the time. For instance, if you want to eat healthier, don't buy junk food. Out of sight means out of mind, and you preserve your willpower for tougher challenges later. Rest matters as much as action. Skipping sleep or pushing yourself too hard drains your focus and self-control. When you make time for breaks, good sleep, and moments to recharge, you actually boost your determination. Think of willpower as a muscle and it needs rest days to grow stronger. Another key lesson is to tackle one habit at a time. Spreading yourself across too many goals at once makes your effort fall flat. Instead, pick one habit maybe drinking more water or writing every day and give it your full attention. After that habit feels natural, add the next one. Each success builds your confidence and energy for the next step. Our brains love patterns. When you repeat an action, it moves from a conscious effort to an automatic routine. That happens in a part of the brain that stores these routines, freeing up mental space for new tasks. This is why, after doing something daily for a while like sitting down to write even a few lines. It feels effortless. Keep showing up consistently, and very soon you'll do it almost without thinking. Every habit follows a simple loop: a cue, the action, and a reward. The cue might be anythin: a time of day, an object you see, or a feeling. The action is the habit itself. And the reward is whatever makes your brain think, "That was good." To build a new habit, pick a clear cue (set your water glass by your bed), do the action (drink), and enjoy a small reward (the refreshing sensation). Tweak these loops until they click. Putting all this together, you begin to see that lasting change doesn't need superhuman effort. It needs smart strategies: choose personal rewards, make progress visible, plan for low-energy days, shape your environment, rest well, focus on one habit, and use clear cues and small steps. Over weeks and months, these small choices build into habits that run on their own so you can live each day with more purpose and ease. Every morning when the sun rises, it doesn't ask for applause. It just rises - quiet, steady, certain. That's how habits grow. Not with fireworks, but with rhythm. Motivation isn't some wild spark that magically makes us productive. It's more like a heartbeat — sometimes strong, sometimes soft, but always present if we listen carefully. People often wait for the "perfect mood" to begin a new habit. But the truth is: moods are like weather - beautiful, but unpredictable. If you wait for sunshine every time, you'll never plant the seed. What works better is **a routine that fits into your life like your favorite old shoe** - comfortable, natural, and reliable. Let's imagine motivation as a traveling friend. Some days, it walks beside you, cheering you on. Other days, it disappears around the corner, leaving you alone. But if your habits are strong enough, you'll keep walking because the path is already familiar. Here's a trick: **talk to yourself like you would to your best friend.** If they slipped up one day, would you say, "You're hopeless!" or "It's okay, try again tomorrow"? Speak to yourself with that same kindness. The habit journey isn't a test of perfection, it's a dance. Miss a step? Just find the rhythm again. You don't need to "feel" motivated to take action. In fact, **action often creates motivation.** Think of lighting a fire not with a spark from the sky, but with your own matchstick. When you begin, even clumsily, your brain wakes up. You start to feel proud. That pride becomes fuel.

Let's take a simple example: stretching. You decide to stretch for 2 minutes each morning. It feels small almost silly. But after a week, you notice something: your posture is better. You breathe easier. You feel calmer. That tiny action is now a signal to your brain: "Hey, we're the kind of person who takes care of our body." This identity shift is magic. **We don't rise to our goals, we fall to our systems.** Many people make the mistake of chasing too much at once. It's like trying to hold ten balloons on a windy day, you'll end up losing all of them. Start with one. Hold it tight. Build trust with yourself. That one habit, once strong, will make room for others. Sometimes, the best way to build a habit is to **attach it to something you already do**. For example, if you drink tea every evening, use that moment to write down one thing you're grateful for. Slowly, that habit sneaks into your life without a fight. You're not changing your routine, you're enriching it and here's something beautiful: **let your habits carry emotion**. Tie them to a purpose that lights your soul. Don't walk just for exercise - walk to clear your thoughts, to reconnect with the sky, to feel the world under your feet. When habits carry meaning, they become easier to keep. One of my favorite ways to stay consistent is to create **rituals, not rules**. A rule sounds cold: "You must do this." But a ritual? A ritual is sacred. Lighting a candle before journaling. Playing soft music while you clean. Smiling at your reflection as you begin the day. These little rituals turn boring tasks into moments of magic. Of course, some days are tough. Life is messy. But here's a secret: even when your routine is shaken, **your comeback matters more than your mistake.** Miss a day? No problem. Return the next day like nothing happened. The real failure is quitting, not slipping. Remember this: **habits are like plants.** You don't dig them up every day to see if they're growing. You water them, protect them, and trust the roots to do their quiet work.

So don't chase perfection. Chase presence.

Don't wait for the fire. Become the match.

Don't look for motivation. Create meaning.

And one day, without even realizing it, you'll look back and see how far you've come not because you were always strong, but because you never stopped showing up. There was a time in my life when I used to think change had to feel grand. Like a movie scene, music swelling, the hero standing on a mountain, shouting their goals to the sky. But real change? It's quieter than that. It's the sound of an early alarm being answered. It's the feeling of brushing your teeth even when you're too tired. It's pouring water into your bottle instead of grabbing a fizzy drink. **Change often begins in silence.** One morning, I watched an old man at the park feed birds with a bag of seeds. Same time, same bench, same smile. I asked him how long he had been doing this. He replied, "Thirty years. It helps me feel grounded." That moment struck me. It wasn't the seeds that mattered. It was the **consistency**. A simple act, repeated over time, became something sacred. A habit.

We often ignore our tiny victories because they don't come with applause. But let me tell you, **your small win today is tomorrow's superpower.** You made your bed? Win. You drank water instead of soda? Win. You read one page of a book? That's momentum. These wins whisper something important: *You're doing better than you think.* You don't need a life overhaul. You need **a few well-placed anchors** - habits that hold you steady when life gets stormy. Think of your day like a boat. Without anchors, the current will take you anywhere. But with just two or three strong habits, you decide your direction. Let's take another example: preparing clothes at night. It sounds boring, right? But here's what happens - your morning begins with **one less decision**. That's energy saved. And saved energy becomes fuel for bigger things - your dreams, your relationships, your growth. I call these *invisible victories.* The world doesn't see them. But your future self will thank you. We live in a world that celebrates speed. But real transformation isn't about sprinting. It's about **showing up again and again, even when it's hard**. It's about learning the rhythm of your life, not someone else's. You don't have to be a morning person. You don't have to journal at 5 a.m. Just **find what fits you** and stay loyal to it.

Here's a little practice that worked wonders for me. I named my habits. Yes, gave them actual names. For example, my walk became "Mind Cleanse." My water bottle routine was called "Fuel Up." Naming made them feel personal like friends, not chores. I felt more connected, and that connection kept me consistent. Also, don't underestimate the power of your **physical space.** A messy desk can make your mind feel foggy. A clean corner can feel like a sanctuary. I used to keep a cluttered workspace until one day, I cleaned it up and added a small plant. That green leaf reminded me daily: growth is slow, but steady. Just like you. Motivation isn't a lightning bolt. It's a **lamp you light every morning**. Some days, the flame is small. Other days, it's brighter. But as long as you protect it, it will never go out. In South Korea, there's an interesting cultural habit around **Jeong**, which is a deep emotional connection and commitment to people and routines. This idea extends to personal habits as well. When something becomes part of your emotional life and community, you stick to it more naturally. For example, many Koreans build exercise habits by joining group classes or community walks. The social bond creates a positive pressure and joy around the habit. From my own experience, sharing goals with friends or family creates a sense of accountability and encouragement, making habits easier to maintain. Spain offers a different yet fascinating approach through the concept of **Siesta**, a short afternoon rest. Although not exactly a habit-building technique, it teaches an important lesson: respecting natural rhythms and not pushing too hard. The idea is that rest isn't a weakness but a strategy for better productivity and well-being. Science agrees. Research from Harvard Medical School shows that short naps can boost memory, creativity, and mood. After adopting a short rest in the afternoon during busy workdays, I noticed my focus and energy improved significantly. Sometimes, building habits means knowing when to pause and recharge.

Combining these lessons from Korea and Spain gives us a richer understanding of how to shape habits. Jeong reminds us of the power of social and emotional support and Siesta shows the importance of rest in sustaining long-term change. Another

Japanese habit worth mentioning is **Shisa Kanko**, which means "looking ahead." It encourages people to visualize the outcomes of their habits and future goals clearly. Visualization is powerful, when you see your success in your mind, your brain starts working toward it. I practice this by imagining how my life will feel after forming a habit. This mental image acts as a guide and motivator during difficult times. In Korea, the practice of **Hwa-byung**, or managing emotional stress, indirectly supports habit formation. Stress and anxiety often cause habit failures, but Koreans use mindfulness and breathing techniques to calm the mind. Incorporating even simple breathing exercises into your daily routine can protect your willpower from being drained by stress. Spain's relaxed approach to meals, called **La Comida**, teaches us to enjoy rituals fully and slow down. When building habits, savoring the process rather than rushing can deepen your connection to the habit, making it more rewarding and lasting.

All these cultural practices highlight an essential truth: habit-building is not only about discipline but about creating a lifestyle that feels natural and fulfilling. These lessons have shaped my own journey and can guide you toward lasting change. Continuing from the lessons of Japan, Korea, and Spain, let's dive deeper into how these cultures handle motivation and setbacks are the two crucial parts of habit formation. In Japan, there is a special concept called **Gambaru**, which roughly means "to do your best" or "to persist." It's a mindset that blends hard work with patience. Unlike rushing to finish a goal quickly, Gambaru teaches steady effort and endurance. This attitude helped me when I faced difficult phases in my learning or work. Instead of giving up, I reminded myself to "keep going" one step at a time, like the Japanese do. This mindset is backed by research on grit, a powerful trait that predicts success better than talent alone. Psychologist Angela Duckworth's studies show that grit is a better predictor of achievement than IQ or raw skill. Gambaru and grit go hand in hand, reminding us that persistence beats instant success. Moving to Korea, the idea of **Han**, a deep feeling of sorrow or unresolved emotion, influences how people deal with failure. Instead of ignoring negative feelings, Koreans acknowledge them and transform pain into strength. This is reflected in their art, music, and even daily life. When habits falter or setbacks occur, embracing the emotion rather than resisting it can be healing and motivating. From my own experience, allowing myself to feel disappointment but then learning from it has made me stronger and more committed. It's not about avoiding failure but growing through it.

Spain brings a different flavor with **Duende**, a term often used in flamenco music to describe a soulful passion and connection to the moment. When habits feel like a chore, passion can fade quickly. Duende teaches us to bring heart and soul into what we do, to find joy even in routine. I have learned that infusing small pleasures or personal meaning into habits makes them stick better. For example, turning exercise into a dance or music session can transform the experience. Studies in psychology support this: people who enjoy their habits are more likely to maintain them long term. Another useful Japanese habit practice is **Mottainai**, a sense of regret over waste. This attitude encourages valuing resources, time, and effort. When building habits, remembering the value of each day and opportunity helps avoid procrastination. Every moment wasted is a chance lost. This practical mindset has helped me respect my time and focus on what matters most. In Korea, the custom of **Jeong** extends beyond emotional ties to include commitment and respect toward oneself. This helps reinforce self-discipline without harsh self-criticism. Balancing kindness with firmness in habit formation creates a nurturing environment for growth. Spain's tradition of **Sobremesa**, the relaxed time after meals spent chatting and bonding, reminds us that community and connection matter. Sharing goals and experiences with loved ones makes habit-building a shared journey, less lonely and more rewarding. These international perspectives enrich the habit-building process with patience, passion, emotional awareness, and community. They show us that habits are not just actions but living parts of our story. Stories that grow stronger with every day's effort. Building habits is much more than just discipline; it's about nurturing a gentle balance between effort and ease. One powerful way to do this is by embracing small, steady progress rather than demanding perfection from the start. Imagine planting a seed. It doesn't grow into a mighty tree overnight. It needs time, water, sunlight, and care. The same goes for habits. When you focus on tiny, daily actions, they quietly build strength beneath the surface. Over time, those actions grow into habits that feel natural, almost like second nature. Another key element is understanding the power of emotions. When you begin a new habit, your mind often swings between excitement and doubt. It's normal to feel frustrated or discouraged when progress slows or slips happen. But instead of pushing those feelings away, try welcoming them. Recognize that every emotion is a signpost on your journey. Sometimes, sadness or frustration points to what needs change, while joy and pride show you what's working. This emotional awareness can be the quiet engine that keeps you moving forward, even when the road feels tough. At the heart of lasting habits lies connection, connection to yourself and those around you. When you treat yourself with kindness and patience, you create a safe space for growth. Harsh self-judgment often leads to giving up. But gentle encouragement helps you rise again after setbacks. Similarly, sharing your goals and struggles with people who care adds layers of support. When others understand your path, their encouragement becomes a lifeline. This connection turns habit-building from a lonely battle into a shared adventure.

Rest and renewal also play a surprising role. While it might seem like pushing harder will speed progress, the truth is that rest fuels endurance. Moments of pause, whether a short break or a peaceful breath, help your brain and body recharge. This makes your efforts more focused and joyful. Think of it as sharpening your tools before continuing the work. It might feel like stopping, but it's really moving forward smarter. Visualizing success is another powerful tool. Picture yourself living with your new habit fully formed, how do you feel? What changes in your life? Creating this mental image lights up your motivation. Your brain begins to believe this future is possible and starts guiding you toward it. This simple act of seeing yourself succeed can be a daily boost that keeps your habit alive.

The magic of habit is in the small joys you build along the way. Find ways to make your habits pleasurable. Maybe it's playing your favorite music while working out or celebrating small wins with a quiet smile. When a habit becomes a source of happiness, it grows roots deep and strong. Over time, these roots hold you steady through challenges and change. In essence, habits are not about forcing yourself to change overnight but weaving new patterns gently into the fabric of your life. They are the quiet, steady steps toward becoming the person you wish to be — patient, resilient, and connected. One of the most beautiful discoveries in behavioral science is the idea that identity shapes action more than willpower ever can. When people see themselves as "someone who exercises" instead of someone who's just "trying to work out," their behavior naturally aligns. It's a shift from doing to becoming. Rather than forcing a habit, you begin to embody it. This idea has been supported by multiple psychological studies — people are more likely to stick to habits when those habits reflect their self-image. Let's take a relatable example. A person who decides, "I want to write every day," might struggle to keep up. But if that person tells themselves, "I am a writer," something changes. Even on hard days, they'll write a sentence or two because that's what writers do. The action becomes part of who they are. And over time, the mind rewires to support this belief. This also connects with a simple technique often used by master craftsmen in traditional communities. They teach through repetition and story rather than rigid rules. Every morning, they don't start with a checklist but with a mindset — they show up with respect for their craft. Their identity as a craftsman keeps them consistent. No alarm clock or external push is needed, the pull comes from within. Another powerful technique found in cultures with strong community rituals is called "anchoring." It's the practice of linking a new habit to something you already do. For example, if you want to practice gratitude, you can do it right after brushing your teeth. Since brushing is already a habit, it becomes the anchor for the new one. You don't need extra willpower — you're just stacking habits. Over time, the new behavior sticks like a leaf joining a growing branch. It's also worth exploring how your surroundings shape your habits. Research shows that people who place their running shoes by the door are far more likely to go for a run than those who keep them in a cupboard. This idea might seem obvious, but it's profound.

Your environment silently influences your behavior all the time. The layout of your room, your desk, your phone, they're either helping or hurting your habits. Try this: if you want to read more, keep a book on your pillow. If you want to drink more water, place a bottle next to your laptop. These are small nudges, but their effects add up. The best part? They require no willpower, just a bit of design thinking. You're setting yourself up to succeed before the moment of decision even arrives. And don't forget the habit of reflection. Taking just five minutes at the end of each day to ask, "What did I do well? What can I improve tomorrow?" builds incredible awareness. It turns every day into a quiet teacher, gently helping you adjust, without judgment. It's not about blaming yourself; it's about learning. So, let your habits be shaped by who you are, by what surrounds you, and by how gently you listen to your days. Let them grow not just in action, but in meaning, until one day, they become a mirror of your soul. There is something deeply powerful about rituals. Not the grand ceremonies, but the small, repeated acts that shape our days. Across cultures, there's a quiet wisdom in starting the day with a structured routine. It could be as simple as making your bed, sipping warm water, or standing silently by the window for a minute before the chaos of life begins. These little things are not just habits, they are anchors of your identity and well-being.

A psychological concept called "implementation intention" helps explain why some people stick to habits while others struggle. It's a mental trick where you decide not just what to do, but when and where you'll do it. For example, instead of saying, "I'll exercise tomorrow," you say, "After I finish breakfast at 8:30 AM, I will go for a 20-minute walk in the park." Studies show that this kind of clarity increases the chance of success by up to 91%. You're turning a vague hope into a real plan. In some communities where people live long and purposeful lives, they often begin the day with a repeatable, meaningful habit. A soft meditation. Tending to a garden. Writing down one thing they're grateful for. These are not just health practices. They are rituals that calm the nervous system and create a rhythm in the mind. You may have noticed it yourself: on days when your morning starts right, everything else flows better. Let me tell you a small story from my life. During a stressful phase of work, I was overwhelmed and restless. I had deadlines piling up, and every morning I woke up feeling like I was already late. It drained me, emotionally and mentally. Then, I decided to do just one thing: write three sentences in a notebook every morning before looking at my phone. No big journaling goal, just three honest lines about how I felt. In a week, I noticed a strange calm. The storm was still there, but I wasn't drowning anymore. That habit became a life-saver. It gave me back my mornings and that's the real point, habits are not about achieving perfection. They are about reclaiming control over your days. The world outside is loud, unpredictable, and demanding. But a habit? That's something you build quietly inside you. You don't need fancy tools or apps. You just need intention and a little time. Interestingly, some traditional systems advise people to design habits that match their body rhythm. For instance, doing mentally demanding tasks in the early hours when the brain is most focused, and creative or spiritual activities during the evening when the mind softens. This natural flow of energy rising and falling helps us work *with* our biology, not against it. So here's something gentle to remember: habits are not about becoming a machine. They are about becoming more *you*. Not harder, just clearer. Not faster, just steadier. Every tiny, repeated action when done with care becomes a thread in the fabric of your life. Do you know what makes a habit last for years? It's not motivation. Motivation is like a visitor, it shows up when it feels like it and leaves without warning. What truly keeps a habit alive is *identity*. When your habit becomes part of who you are, it sticks. It becomes something you no longer have to force because it feels natural. Let's imagine two people trying to quit smoking. One says, "I'm trying to quit." The other says, "I'm not a smoker." See the difference? The first is struggling against a habit. The second has already shifted their identity. The brain follows the story we tell about ourselves.

When we say, "I'm a reader," we pick up books more often. When we say, "I'm healthy," we are more likely to choose nourishing food. Identity drives action and action, repeated, becomes identity. It's a beautiful circle. Some research in behavioral science explains that the most sustainable habits are built not by big changes, but by *tiny wins*. A fascinating study showed that people who started with flossing just one tooth daily were more likely to stick to dental hygiene than those who were told to floss all teeth. Why? Because one tooth is easy. It doesn't feel like a mountain to climb. And often, once we start small, we naturally do more.

That's why habits that feel too big often fail. We start with excitement, reading for an hour, running five kilometers, eating no sugar but the excitement fades after sometime. The habit then becomes a burden. The key is to make the habit so easy that it feels silly *not* to do it. One push-up. One page. One deep breath. These are seeds. They grow slowly, but steadily.

Let me share something I've learned through experience. At a time when I was struggling to stay productive, I created a "one-minute rule." If a task would take less than one minute, I did it immediately whether it was replying to a message, putting away my shoes, or jotting down an idea. That single habit reduced clutter in my mind and environment. It wasn't dramatic, but it was powerful. Another wonderful habit-building trick comes from a method called "habit stacking." You take an existing habit like something you do without thinking and attach a new habit to it. For example, "After I make my morning tea, I will write down one goal for the day." Since the tea habit already exists, it becomes the anchor for the new one. Over time, the new habit rides on the back of the old one. Most of us don't lack discipline. We simply lack *systems*. If you have to think too much about when and how to act, you'll probably skip it. But if your habit is part of a pattern, part of your environment, and tied to your sense of self, it becomes automatic. That's how great habits are born not from pressure, but from design. So, start small. Make it easy. Attach it to your identity. Let it grow in the background like a seed planted with love. Do you remember the first time you brushed your teeth by yourself? Probably not. Yet, it's something you do every day without even thinking. That's the magic of habit. It becomes invisible, but powerful. It becomes part of the rhythm of your life. Now, what if we could turn other powerful actions like journaling, deep breathing, or practicing gratitude into this same kind of automatic behavior? In my own journey, this changed everything. I used to say, "I'll study more," but often failed. Then I changed it to: "At 8 PM, I will revise for 30 minutes at my study table." The shift was almost magical. The moment the clock hit 8, my body knew what to do. It's like giving your brain a shortcut. There's also a deeply human side to habits, our emotional connection. Habits that make us *feel good* are more likely to stick. That's why reward is a crucial part of habit loops. If you feel happy after stretching in the morning, your brain remembers the pleasure and encourages repetition. But if a habit feels like punishment, we avoid it. So the key? Make your habits emotionally rewarding. Pair your evening walk with your favorite music. Treat yourself to a warm drink after writing your journal entry. Celebrate your small wins.

Another smart technique is visual habit tracking. A simple calendar where you tick a box every day you complete a habit. Over time, seeing those ticks creates a chain, and your brain wants to keep it going. It's satisfying. It's visual proof that you're moving forward.

But let me tell you — missing a day isn't failure. Life isn't perfect. The real trick is this: never miss two days in a row. Forgive yourself quickly. Then come back with love. Habits built with patience are habits that last.

So remember, habits are not cages, they are wings. They don't confine you, they carry you. So give yourself time. Trust the process. Keep walking the path.

5. The Science of Starting Again

We often carry a quiet burden, a fear of starting over. Whether it's restarting a career, fixing a broken routine, or rebuilding confidence after failure, the idea of beginning again feels like defeat. But what if we've been looking at it all wrong? What if *starting again* is actually the most courageous, most intelligent thing a person can do?

In behavioral psychology, there's a fascinating concept called the **"fresh start effect."** Researchers have found that people are more likely to begin meaningful changes at natural time points like the start of a week, a month, or a birthday. It's not because anything magical happens on a Monday or January 1st. It's because the brain sees these points as psychological "resets." They help us separate our past selves from our future selves. This concept is powerful because it shows that change isn't tied to grand moments. You don't have to wait for a new year to change your life. You can declare a "fresh start" on a Wednesday afternoon. What matters isn't the timing, it's the mindset. Let's take a real example. I once met someone who failed in a business he put years into. For six months, he didn't want to try again. He felt defeated, ashamed. But then he gave himself a "clean page" day. He took a notebook, wrote down only *one* thing he wanted to do differently. That small act, repeated daily, became his blueprint to a new business stronger and smarter than before. It didn't rise from inspiration. It rose from *permission.* Permission to begin again. Neuroscience supports this. The **prefrontal cortex**, the part of the brain responsible for decision-making, thrives when we feel agency - when we believe we *can* act. When we label a new beginning as possible, we literally activate the part of the brain that helps us commit and stay focused. That's not just poetic, it's biological. But here's the beautiful twist. Starting again doesn't mean you failed. It means you grew. Growth means your old version is outdated. Think of it like a phone update when things improve, you restart. That doesn't make the previous version useless, it just makes the new one better. So if you've been stuck, paused, or afraid to try again, remember this: life isn't a straight road. It's a spiral staircase. Sometimes we return to the same point, but at a higher level. That's not failure. That's *elevation.*

The journey of starting again often feels like walking into a fog - uncertain, unfamiliar, and lonely. But scientists have discovered that this uncertainty is also where the greatest growth happens. Psychologists call this period the **"zone of proximal development."** It's a space where you're no longer where you were, but you haven't yet reached where you want to be. It's uncomfortable, yes but also fertile. Research from developmental psychology shows that when we embrace this space, instead of rushing past it or avoiding it, our brains build stronger neural connections. These connections are the physical foundation of new skills, new habits, and new ways of thinking. The brain, in a sense, rewards courage in uncertainty. Think about a child learning to walk. They fall many times, but each fall rewires their brain a little more for balance and coordination. The child doesn't see failure - only progress. That same patience is essential for anyone starting again in life. In one study published in *Frontiers in Psychology* (2019), researchers found that people who viewed setbacks as learning opportunities were far more likely to recover quickly and succeed long-term than those who saw failure as a fixed end. Now, this isn't just theory. From my own life and the lives of people I've met, the moments of greatest restart have often been cloaked in fear and self-doubt. But those who gave themselves permission to be imperfect, to be slow, and to be curious, found unexpected strength. For example, during my early days at my Company, I struggled with new responsibilities. I made mistakes, some big enough to shake my confidence. But I learned to treat every mistake as a "data point", a piece of information to guide my next step. Instead of avoiding failure, I welcomed it as part of the process. This shift helped me grow faster and deeper than any smooth success could have. There is also a practical method to help during restarts: the **"small win strategy."** A study from the University of Chicago showed that even tiny achievements can create a positive feedback loop in our brain, releasing dopamine, This means celebrating the smallest victories, like sending an email, completing a short task, or simply showing up. These wins make the fog clearer and the path more visible. So, the science and the stories tell us: starting again is a sacred act of courage. It rewires your brain, it builds resilience, and it connects you to your own inner power. It's okay to feel scared. It's okay to feel unsure. But in those moments, you are becoming stronger. When we face the challenge of starting over, many of us wrestle with a hidden enemy: **perfectionism**. It disguises itself as a quest for excellence, but often, it becomes the reason we hesitate to take the first step. The fear of not being perfect can freeze us in place, making the fresh start seem impossible. Scientific studies on creativity and productivity reveal that waiting for the "perfect moment" or the "perfect plan" is actually a major barrier to progress. But the truth that many don't realize: **the act of beginning, even imperfectly, reshapes the brain in ways perfection never can.** Think of it like gardening. Waiting for the "perfect soil" or "ideal weather" before planting seeds means the garden never grows. But planting anyway — adjusting, nurturing, and learning as you go will yield blooms. The gardener's patience and willingness to begin despite imperfect conditions bring life to the garden. In my own experience, early in my career, I was caught in the trap of over-planning. I would wait for every detail to be "just right." What I learned, painfully, was that **waiting delayed my growth far more than failure ever could**. When I finally took imperfect action, the momentum built quickly. Each step forward made the next step easier and clearer. Researchers studying habits have found that **action itself creates motivation**. This is called the "activation energy". In psychology, the initial push that ignites change. Surprisingly, once you take that first small step, your brain releases chemicals that reward you and encourage continuation. Waiting for motivation before starting is a myth; motivation often follows action. This idea explains why so many successful people emphasize "just start." The power is not in waiting for the perfect moment but in creating your own momentum through imperfect action. Imagine a small spark lighting a dark room. That spark doesn't need to be a roaring fire immediately. But it opens the space for warmth and light to grow. Your first step is that spark. So, the secret to starting again is to let go of perfection. Let go of the idea that you must have all answers. Embrace the messy, beautiful process of learning as you go. It is in this act that true growth and transformation lie. One of the most powerful yet overlooked truths about starting again is the role of **self-compassion**. Often, when we falter or face setbacks, our inner voice becomes harsh and unforgiving. This inner criticism can deepen our fear and hesitation, making new beginnings feel even more daunting.

But science tells us a different story, one where kindness to ourselves becomes a catalyst for change. Research by Dr. Kristin Neff, a leading expert on self-compassion, shows that people who treat themselves with warmth and understanding during difficult times recover faster and approach new challenges with greater confidence. When you replace harsh judgment with gentle encouragement, your brain's stress response calms down. This allows you to think more clearly, plan better, and take courageous steps forward. Self-compassion is not about excusing mistakes or avoiding responsibility. Instead, it's about recognizing that failure, fear, and struggle are part of the shared human experience. This recognition connects us to a deeper sense of belonging and reduces feelings of isolation, which often accompany the need to start over. In my personal journey, I remember a time when a big project at work didn't go as planned. My first instinct was to criticize myself harshly, to replay every error in my mind. But slowly, I learned to pause and speak to myself as I would to a close friend: with kindness and patience. This shift changed everything. The pressure eased, and I could see solutions where before there were only obstacles. Interestingly, research in neuroscience supports this. When we practice self-compassion, areas of the brain linked to emotional regulation and reward light up. This means that kindness to ourselves is literally rewiring our brain for resilience. Starting again is never easy. But when you carry yourself with kindness, you create a safe inner space from which courage naturally emerges. It's like planting a seed in rich, nurturing soil, the chances of growth become much stronger.

So as you face your fresh start, remember: your greatest ally is not perfection or endless motivation. It is the compassionate voice within, quietly urging you forward, reminding you that you are worthy of success, no matter how many times you begin again. A study conducted by Dr. Teresa Amabile at Harvard Business School revealed that people who recognize even small progress in their efforts feel more motivated, confident, and satisfied. When I started my job, I was overwhelmed by the sheer amount of knowledge I had to gain and the skills I needed to build. Instead of focusing on the daunting whole, I set mini-goals: mastering one new software function each day or learning a new term every morning. Celebrating these small victories kept me motivated even on tough days. Psychologically, this process works because the brain rewards progress. Every small success releases dopamine, a neurotransmitter that creates feelings of pleasure and reinforces behavior. This positive feedback loop makes us eager to continue, transforming what could be exhausting into something energizing.

Seeing progress visually is a powerful reminder that you are moving forward, step by step. Interestingly, this approach is ranged in many traditional techniques around the world. Whether in arts, crafts, or sports, mastery comes not from giant leaps but consistent, incremental improvement. The ancient wisdom behind these practices is now supported by modern science. So, as you face the challenge of starting anew, remember this: success is not a giant leap but a series of small, steady steps. Each step builds your confidence, strengthens your skills, and brings your dreams closer to reality. With patience, kindness, and focus on small wins, you can turn the fear of starting over into an exciting journey filled with discovery and growth. A powerful but often overlooked tool for beginning again is the art of **reframing failure**. When things don't go as planned, many of us instinctively see failure as a dead end, a label of "I'm not good enough." But what if failure is not the enemy, but a guidepost? What if every failure is simply a lesson disguised in a hard moment? Psychologists have studied how our mindset about failure shapes our ability to bounce back. Carol Dweck's work on growth mindset shows that when we view abilities as learnable and flexible, setbacks become opportunities rather than obstacles. This mindset transforms failure from a source of shame to a stepping stone on the path of growth. I recall a time early in my career when a project I deeply cared about did not succeed. Initially, I was crushed and doubted my skills. But over time, I shifted my view. I started asking, "What can this teach me? How can I improve?" This change in perspective opened doors I hadn't seen before and led me to new skills and connections. Science backs this up. Practically, you can start reframing failure by keeping a "learning journal." After every setback, write down what happened, what you learned, and one small step you can take next. This simple habit rewires your brain to seek growth, not guilt.

This approach is quietly practiced in many cultures through storytelling and rituals that honor mistakes as natural parts of life. Such wisdom encourages us to embrace imperfection and keep trying, even when the road is tough. Remember, starting again is rarely about avoiding failure. It's about growing stronger because of it. Every misstep is a lesson, every stumble a chance to rise more skilled and more resilient. This mindset frees you from the fear of failing, giving you the courage to take the first step, again and again. One often unnoticed but vital part of beginning again is the role of **rituals**—small, meaningful actions that help us transition from one phase of life to another. Rituals can be as simple as lighting a candle, writing a letter to yourself, or even taking a quiet walk in nature. These actions may seem small, but they carry immense power to center the mind, calm the heart, and prepare the spirit for change.

Neuroscience shows that rituals engage the brain's pattern-seeking nature. They provide structure and predictability, which reduce anxiety during uncertain times. When we perform a ritual, our brain releases feel-good chemicals like dopamine and serotonin, helping us feel safe and focused. From my experience, starting a new chapter in life often felt overwhelming, full of doubt and hesitation. But creating small personal rituals helped me mark these transitions. For example, I developed a habit of journaling three things I was grateful for each morning before diving into work. This simple ritual shifted my mindset from worry to appreciation, making it easier to face challenges.

Many ancient and modern cultures also recognize the power of rituals to heal and renew. These practices build a bridge between the past and future, helping us release old patterns and welcome new possibilities. A beautiful aspect of rituals is that they don't require grand gestures. Even a few minutes of deep breathing, a cup of tea enjoyed mindfully, or tidying your workspace can become a sacred pause, a moment of renewal. So, when you find yourself needing to start over, try creating your own rituals, small acts that give you comfort, clarity, and courage. These rituals become anchors, steadying you amid the uncertainty of new beginnings. The science and experience both agree: rituals are not just traditions; they are tools to help the heart open and the mind focus, making every fresh start a little easier to embrace. Another key element in the art of starting again is learning to accept **uncertainty**. It's natural to want clear answers, stable paths, and guaranteed outcomes. Yet, life rarely offers these comforts when we begin anew. Instead, uncertainty becomes the ground on which growth and transformation happen.

Research in psychology points to the importance of becoming comfortable with uncertainty. Studies show that people who tolerate ambiguity and unpredictability are more creative, resilient, and open to new experiences. This doesn't mean ignoring risks, but rather accepting that not everything can be controlled or predicted.

In my own journey, I learned this lesson slowly. I often felt anxious about unknown outcomes. But gradually, I realized that uncertainty was not my enemy. Instead, it was a signal that I was stepping outside my comfort zone into a space where real growth happens.

Interestingly, mindfulness practices support this idea. By focusing on the present moment without judgment, mindfulness trains the mind to accept whatever arises whether comfort or discomfort, clarity or confusion. This skill reduces the fear of uncertainty and helps us move forward with calm confidence. In cultures where uncertainty is embraced, people often use storytelling, meditation, or community support to face unknown futures together. These shared practices strengthen individuals' courage and sense of belonging. So when you feel overwhelmed by the unknown, remember: uncertainty is the soil in which new possibilities grow. Rather than resist it, lean into it with curiosity and openness. This mindset shift transforms fear into excitement and hesitation into hope. Life's most meaningful changes start in uncertainty. The courage to begin again grows when we learn to dance with the unknown rather than run from it. Research in behavioral science confirms this approach. The "progress principle" tells us that making small achievements boosts motivation and happiness far more than waiting for one big success. I remember a time when I faced a major career shift. The entire process seemed daunting, and I almost froze in hesitation. Then, I decided to set one small goal every day like learning a new skill for 15 minutes or connecting with one new person. Over weeks, these small goals built momentum, confidence, and eventually, real change. Many cultures honor the power of gradual progress. Ancient craftspeople would focus on perfecting one tiny detail of their work at a time, knowing that mastery is built step by step. Similarly, modern habits like the "one percent improvement" encourage us to get just a little better every day. This method also helps combat the perfectionism trap. When you focus on small steps, mistakes become less scary because you can adjust quickly. You learn to value effort and persistence over immediate perfection. Remember, great journeys aren't made in leaps alone; they are crafted with many small, meaningful steps that transform fear into progress and hope into reality. Starting again often means redefining what success truly means to us. In the rush of modern life, we often equate success with fame, wealth, or fast results. But research on human happiness and fulfillment reveals a richer truth: success is deeply personal and tied to a sense of purpose and well-being. Psychologists studying happiness find that people who define success by connection, growth, and meaning tend to experience more lasting joy. This isn't just theory, it's supported by real stories from people who chose passion over paycheck or learning over status.

In my own life, moments when I focused solely on external achievements often left me feeling empty. But when I shifted focus to how I could grow, contribute, and find joy in small moments, my sense of success deepened. What does success mean to you? Is it a title, a bank balance, or something more quiet and profound like peace of mind or time with loved ones? How might your life change if you redefined success on your own terms? Taking time to answer these questions can help you create a fresh start with clarity and heart. This clarity becomes a compass, guiding your steps forward through uncertainty. When we start over, one surprising factor plays a huge role - **our environment**. Scientists who study behavior change highlight how the spaces around us influence our habits, mindset, and motivation. A cluttered room can clutter the mind. A calm, inspiring space can fuel creativity and courage. Have you noticed how your surroundings affect your mood? Could a simple change in your environment support your fresh start? Researchers call this the "choice architecture" designing your environment so the good habits are easier and the distractions harder. For example, placing a journal on your bedside table nudges you to write. Turning off notifications helps your mind stay calm. If you want to start again, try shaping your space to support the new path you choose. It's like planting seeds in fertile soil, the right environment helps you grow stronger and faster. One of the most overlooked yet powerful elements in starting fresh is the environment we surround ourselves with. Our physical space like the rooms we live in, the objects we see, the sounds we hear deeply influences our thoughts, emotions, and behaviors. This isn't just a poetic idea; it's backed by science. Behavioral scientists explain this through the concept of **"choice architecture."** This means that small details in our environment can nudge us toward better choices without us even realizing it. For example, having a water bottle within arm's reach encourages hydration. Keeping your workspace tidy and organized can make focusing easier. On the other hand, a cluttered, noisy room can drain your energy and scatter your thoughts. In one fascinating study, researchers found that people who kept their desks clean and neat were more productive and less stressed compared to those with cluttered workspaces. Even simple changes, like natural light streaming through windows, plants that bring nature indoors, or playing soft, calming music, can boost mood and creativity. In my own life, I have seen this clearly. During times when I felt stuck or overwhelmed, changing my surroundings even in small ways helped me regain clarity and courage. For instance, opening the windows for fresh air, lighting a candle with a comforting scent, or sitting in a quiet park made a surprising difference. These shifts weren't magic, but they created an atmosphere where my mind felt safe to explore new ideas and take risks. Ask yourself: How do your current surroundings make you feel? Are they helping you grow, or holding you back? Could a simple change like clearing a corner, adding a favorite photo, or stepping outside more often support your fresh start? This concept is also tied to ancient traditions. Many cultures have long recognized the importance of sacred or peaceful spaces, places designed to calm the mind and inspire the soul. Think of meditation rooms, gardens, or even the simple act of lighting incense or arranging flowers. These practices show how intentional spaces can ground us and provide strength during new beginnings. In practical terms, shaping your environment is about making good habits easier to follow and bad habits harder to slip into. For example, if you want to read more, keep a book on your pillow or desk where you'll see it often. If you want to eat healthier, place fruits and nuts where they are visible, while storing tempting snacks out of sight. The environment gently guides your choices without demanding willpower.

Changing your surroundings is an act of self-care and empowerment. It sends a message to your brain: "This place supports my goals and dreams." When you create such a space, you are planting seeds in fertile soil and those seeds will grow into new strengths, habits, and joys. So, as you prepare for a fresh start, consider your environment as a powerful ally. What small changes can you make today to invite calm, focus, and motivation into your life? Your surroundings can become the quiet champion that helps you rise again.Starting again isn't just about the mind — the body plays a crucial role too. Our physical health, energy levels, and daily rhythms shape how we feel and what we can achieve. Scientific research shows that even small changes in our daily movement and breathing patterns can powerfully reset our mental and emotional state. Have you ever noticed how a short walk in fresh air can clear your mind? Or how deep breaths can calm racing thoughts? This is because movement and breath directly affect the nervous system, the body's communication network. The nervous system governs how we respond to stress, focus on tasks, and regulate emotions. In fact, a growing field called **somatic science** studies how body awareness can help release stress and support mental clarity. For centuries, traditional practices like yoga, tai chi, and mindful breathing have understood this connection intuitively. Now modern science confirms that gentle, intentional movement wakes up the body's natural healing and calming systems. From personal experience, when I felt overwhelmed by work or life challenges, pausing for a few minutes of deep breathing or stretching helped me find balance. This simple pause created space in my busy mind and recharged my focus. It was a small act, yet it changed my whole day. Scientific studies also tell us that the vagus nerve, a major nerve connecting the brain and body plays a key role in regulating this calm. Stimulating the vagus nerve through slow breathing, humming, or even cold water on the face can switch the body from a stressed "fight or flight" state to a relaxed "rest and digest" mode. Imagine this: you are about to start a new chapter in your life. Before diving in, you take a moment to sit quietly, breathe deeply, and gently move your body. This simple ritual signals to your nervous system that you are safe, ready, and open to growth. This body-mind harmony is often overlooked but is essential for fresh starts. When the body feels calm and energized, the mind naturally follows. This creates a powerful foundation to build new habits, face challenges, and stay motivated. Have you tried to begin something new when your body felt tired or tense? How was that experience? It's tough because our body and mind are deeply linked — when one struggles, the other often follows. This is why self-care isn't selfish; it's necessary. So, as you prepare to start again, consider tuning into your body. Notice your posture, breath, and energy. Small daily practices like stretching in the morning, walking outdoors, or mindful breathing can ground you and open your heart to possibility. Resilience is often painted as a heroic return to form a glorious comeback where everything looks polished again. But real resilience isn't dramatic or loud. It's quiet, internal, and deeply human. It's what happens in the small, uncelebrated moments, when you decide to try again after rejection, when you get out of bed with a heavy heart, or when you choose to believe in yourself even though everything around you says otherwise. It's not the victory lap that defines resilience, it's the decision to keep walking when there's no cheering crowd. And what's more compelling is that resilience isn't something you're born with in fixed quantity. It's a living, evolving skill is a psychological muscle that grows stronger with every honest encounter with hardship. The mind, contrary to popular belief, is not a fixed vessel. Neuroscience has shattered that myth. What we know now is powerful: the human brain remains plastic throughout life. Neuroplasticity allows the brain to rewire itself through intentional thought, behavior, and repetition. That means resilience isn't something you inherit. It's something you build, moment by moment, choice by choice. Each time you challenge a negative thought or sit with discomfort without numbing it, you're physically altering the wiring of your brain. That's not just metaphorical strength, it's biological transformation and yet, our cultural obsession with perfection often robs us of the gift of resilience. We are taught to celebrate success and hide struggle, to curate our lives like highlight reels and bury our pain beneath filters and smiles. But true resilience grows in the messy, unedited moments. In the hospital waiting room. In the apology after a failed relationship. In the second attempt after the first falls flat. Resilience is forged in the fire of lived experience, not imagined perfection. And ironically, the more we embrace the cracks in our stories, the stronger and more luminous our character becomes. Think of a Japanese art form called Kintsugi, where broken pottery is repaired using gold lacquer. The philosophy isn't to hide the break, it's to honor it. The repaired piece isn't seen as damaged but as more beautiful for having been broken. That's what resilience is: not the hiding of scars, but the highlighting of them. They tell a story of someone who didn't quit. Someone who dared to continue. Someone who chose to shine not despite their wounds, but through them. This truth finds echo in countless lives. A woman in her fifties, after battling cancer and losing her job, decides to go back to university and study psychology, something she had shelved decades earlier. A young man, devastated by a startup failure, uses that loss to launch a support group for first-time entrepreneurs. A mother, grieving the death of a child, creates a foundation that helps others in pain find meaning again. What's striking is that these people didn't wait for perfect timing. They began in the middle of the mess. And that's a key insight: resilience isn't about waiting for the storm to pass, it's about learning to dance in the rain. It's about saying, "Even now, I will try." That willingness opens doors not only in the outside world but within the self. Because every act of trying again reinforces the belief that you are not finished yet that your story is still being written and writing your story, in the truest sense, means giving yourself the authority to reinterpret the events of your life. That doesn't mean ignoring pain or glossing over wounds. It means deciding what those experiences will mean. Will that heartbreak define you as broken? Or will it become the chapter where you discovered self-worth? Will that failure be your ending, or the moment you rewrote your definition of success?

There is something extraordinary that happens when you choose to stand back up. Not just physically, but emotionally and mentally. Scientists have studied the biology of recovery and found that the human body is designed to heal. But what's even more fascinating is that the human mind is not only designed to recover. It's designed to evolve through the experience. When we go through a crisis, whether it's emotional heartbreak, job loss, illness, or even existential confusion, the brain activates something called the **salience network**. This network acts like an internal spotlight, helping us detect what matters most in that moment of chaos. In simpler terms, pain forces us to re-evaluate, to prioritize, to ask, "What do I truly care about now?" And in that deep questioning, something magical begins. We begin to change, not just on the surface, but at our very core. The hippocampus, which is involved in memory and learning, our emotional alarm system to help us process trauma. When we sit with our discomfort instead of running from it, we begin to transform the raw memory into understanding. And understanding is what unlocks strength. This process is called "emotional integration." It's like stitching the torn fabric of your identity back together not to make it look like it did before, but to create something even stronger than before. That is why people who have gone through deep suffering often emerge with an almost unshakable calm. They have walked through their storm. They know its power. And more importantly, they've found out that they could survive it. Resilience isn't born from untouched lives. It comes from those who have faced the hurricane and decided not to be swept away. In 2004, a psychologist named Dr. George Bonanno introduced the idea of **"resilience trajectories."** He found that people respond to adversity in different patterns, some bounce back quickly, others take time, and some show delayed growth. What mattered most, however, was not how fast people recovered, but that they **allowed themselves to feel**. They cried. They broke. They questioned. But they never lost the belief that healing was possible. And that belief, more than anything else, was the key. This belief, this inner compass that points us toward healing even in the darkest moments, is more powerful than we realize. In fact, studies in **positive psychology**, especially the work of Dr. Martin Seligman, have shown that people who cultivate **hope**, not blind optimism, but grounded, intentional hope are more likely to recover from setbacks and live fulfilling lives. Hope is not naïve. It is a discipline. It is the quiet decision to believe in the possibility of light, even when you're surrounded by night. And that decision can literally reshape the brain. In neuroimaging studies, hope activates regions of the brain associated with **planning, goal-setting, and action-taking**. In other words, when you decide to believe that life can be different, your brain starts building a path toward that future. But how do we keep believing when life has stripped us bare? When the losses feel unbearable, and the future looks like a fog? This is where **meaning** enters the picture. Viktor Frankl, a Holocaust survivor and psychiatrist, wrote that humans can endure almost any "how" if they have a strong enough "why." He discovered, even in the concentration camps, that those who found meaning in love, in faith, in helping others were more likely to survive. Meaning acts as a spiritual anchor. It doesn't remove the pain, but it gives you something bigger to hold onto when the pain threatens to drown you. It's like a lighthouse during a storm. You might still be tossed by the waves, but at least you have a direction. A reason to keep swimming. Modern psychology confirms this. Research in **logotherapy** and **existential psychology** shows that people who are guided by values like honesty, compassion, courage, service tend to recover from trauma with a deeper sense of self. These values act like guardrails, guiding you back when life has derailed your plans. You may lose a job, a relationship, or even your health, but your values remind you of who you still are. They are the unchanging stars in your emotional sky. And they help you remember that you are more than what has happened to you. You are what you choose to become, starting from here.There's also a growing field of research around **compassion resilience**, which shows that when we extend kindness not just to others but to ourselves - we build emotional immunity. Think about it: when your best friend fails, you don't call them a loser or tell them they'll never succeed. You comfort them. You remind them of their worth. But how often do we do that for ourselves? Most of us have an inner critic so loud and cruel that it drowns out any voice of hope. Learning to speak to yourself with compassion saying, "It's okay to be here. It's okay to not have it figured out. I am still worthy." this is not weakness. It's emotional strength. It's what helps the brain shift from survival mode to growth mode. Neuroscience proves it: **self-compassion reduces cortisol**, the stress hormone, and increases **oxytocin**, the bonding hormone. So being kind to yourself is not only comforting, it's chemically healing and perhaps the most powerful aspect of resilience is this: it is contagious. When you rise, when you heal, when you share your story not as a victim but as a survivor, you give others silent permission to do the same. You never know who is watching. A younger sibling. A colleague. A stranger who reads your words or hears your voice.

Every act of choosing to heal sends out a ripple. It changes more than just your life. It changes the atmosphere around you. And over time, these ripples form waves of hope, big enough to carry others too.

So if you're in the middle of rebuilding, if you've lost something, or someone, or maybe even lost a part of yourself, let this be your reminder: you're not starting from nothing. You're starting from experience. From grit,from truth and every day you choose to keep going, you're not just surviving, you're evolving. You are sculpting a new version of yourself with hands that have already learned how to mend. That is not weakness.

That is wisdom in motion. Let resilience not be the thing you reach for only when everything breaks. Let it be the quiet, constant fire that burns in your chest reminding you that no matter what comes, you have already faced storms. And you are still here. Not the same, but deeper. Not untouched, but more complete. You are the proof that broken things don't just get repaired, they get redesigned.

6. Be Your Own Coach

In life's journey, one of the most empowering skills you can develop is learning to coach yourself. This means becoming your own guide, mentor, and motivator, all rolled into one. Coaching psychology offers profound insights and practical methods that, when applied to yourself, can transform your mindset and daily habits. Unlike traditional advice that often emphasizes external validation or dependence on others, being your own coach nurtures self-reliance and deeper self-awareness. It unlocks the power to set meaningful goals, track your progress effectively, and reignite motivation even in challenging moments. Coaching psychology is a modern, evidence-based field that combines the science of psychology with the art of personal development. At its core, coaching psychology focuses on facilitating growth through reflective questioning, goal clarity, and accountability elements you can incorporate into your self-coaching practice. Research shows that people who actively engage in self-coaching demonstrate higher resilience, improved emotional regulation, and greater achievement across life domains. This chapter explores how to harness those techniques and implement tools that will track your journey toward self-mastery. One foundational idea from coaching psychology is the power of **self-reflective questioning**. Rather than rushing to solve problems, asking yourself open-ended questions encourages curiosity and insight. For example, instead of thinking, "Why am I failing?" try asking, "What can I learn from this experience?" or "What resources do I have that I haven't yet considered?" This subtle shift in language helps pivot your mindset from judgment and defeat to exploration and solution-building. The questions you ask yourself become the compass that directs your mental energy toward growth rather than stagnation.

Another technique is goal-setting grounded in the SMART framework which is Specific, Measurable, Achievable, Relevant, and Time-bound. Coaching psychology research confirms that well-structured goals significantly increase the chances of success by making your intentions concrete. But beyond just setting goals, the real magic happens when you break those goals into micro-steps. These micro-steps serve as mini-milestones, allowing frequent celebrations of progress and preventing overwhelm. When coaching yourself, you become both the planner and the cheerleader, recognizing small wins that build momentum over time.

The principle of **accountability** also plays a pivotal role in self-coaching. Many people struggle to follow through because they lack someone to report their progress to. When you coach yourself, establishing a system of accountability is crucial. This might involve journaling daily reflections, setting reminders for check-ins, or even using digital apps designed to track habits and goals. Research indicates that externalizing accountability writing down your commitments or sharing them with even a small circle dramatically improves follow-through. You can simulate this effect internally by creating rituals where you review and adjust your goals regularly.

Emotional regulation techniques from coaching psychology also enhance self-coaching efficacy. Learning to recognize and manage emotions such as frustration, fear, or self-doubt can prevent derailment. Tools like mindfulness meditation, deep breathing exercises, and cognitive reframing empower you to stay present and objective, rather than reactive. Studies demonstrate that individuals who master emotional regulation experience higher motivation and sustain effort longer, which is vital when coaching yourself through setbacks.

To sum up this introduction, being your own coach is not about harsh self-criticism or unrealistic perfection. It's a compassionate, structured approach to guiding your own growth through powerful questioning, clear goal-setting, consistent accountability, and emotional intelligence. The pages ahead will unpack these techniques and tools in greater detail, giving you a robust, practical blueprint for turning your dreams into achievable realities all driven by the unstoppable force within: you. Diving deeper into the science behind self-coaching, it's essential to understand how the brain supports or sabotages our ability to motivate and achieve. Neuroscience research reveals that coaching techniques tap into the brain's executive functions those cognitive processes responsible for planning, attention, and self-control. When you become your own coach, you essentially train these functions to work cohesively rather than in conflict. This means that habits, mindsets, and emotional patterns aren't fixed. They can be reshaped with consistent practice. Studies by renowned neuroscientists like Dr. Norman Doidge demonstrate that intentional, repetitive behaviors, such as those cultivated through coaching techniques, physically alter brain pathways. This rewiring supports better problem-solving, emotional regulation, and sustained motivation.

Key to this process is **metacognition**. Thinking about your own thinking. In coaching, metacognition allows you to step outside automatic reactions and observe your thought patterns objectively. For example, if you notice a recurring negative thought like "I can't do this," metacognition helps you catch that thought early and question its validity. Research in educational psychology shows that metacognitive strategies improve learning outcomes, self-efficacy, and resilience. When coaching yourself, developing metacognitive awareness is akin to having an internal coach who guides you toward smarter, more adaptive thinking.

Another critical aspect of self-coaching is understanding **motivation theories** to keep yourself engaged. According to the Self-Determination Theory (SDT) developed by Deci and Ryan, motivation exists along a spectrum from extrinsic (external rewards or pressure) to intrinsic (internal satisfaction and meaning). Intrinsic motivation is the holy grail of sustainable progress. As your own coach, your goal is to cultivate intrinsic motivation by aligning your objectives with your core values and sense of purpose. Numerous studies confirm that when goals resonate personally, you're more likely to persist despite obstacles. Alongside motivation, **goal-setting theory** by psychologist Edwin Locke highlights that goals must be challenging yet attainable to maximize performance. Locke's research found that vague or easy goals result in poor effort and lower achievement, whereas specific, difficult goals push individuals to excel. This theory reinforces why coaching psychology emphasizes the SMART goal framework and micro-goals: they provide clarity and stretch your capabilities without setting you up for failure.

A practical coaching tool informed by research is the **GROW model**, originally developed in executive coaching but highly adaptable for self-coaching. GROW stands for Goal, Reality, Options, and Will (or Way Forward). By systematically working through these stages, you gain clarity on where you want to go, understand your current situation without distortion, explore creative solutions, and commit to specific actions. Studies show that structured frameworks like GROW enhance decision-making and behavioral change by reducing overwhelm and increasing focus. Tracking your progress is another research-backed pillar of effective self-coaching. Behavioral science underscores the importance of feedback loops in learning and habit formation. The famous psychologist B.F. Skinner demonstrated through operant conditioning that timely, consistent feedback whether rewards or constructive adjustments strengthens our desired behaviors. When you monitor your actions and outcomes regularly, you create a feedback loop that propels growth. Technologies such as habit-tracking apps and journaling act as digital or analog mirrors, reflecting your efforts back to you and enabling timely course corrections. Beyond just quantitative tracking, **qualitative self-reflection** is equally vital. Journaling, for instance, is linked to reduced stress, increased emotional intelligence, and clearer goal articulation. Psychologist James Pennebaker's research reveals that expressive writing helps process complex emotions and solidify intentions. Writing about your daily experiences as your own coach allows you to detect patterns, celebrate breakthroughs, and troubleshoot obstacles with a calm, curious mindset. Together, these neuroscience and psychology insights form a powerful foundation for self-coaching. By understanding how your brain works, what motivates you, and how to structure your goals and feedback effectively, you equip yourself with a science-backed system for sustainable growth. First, the **Daily Reflection Journal** is a simple yet transformative tool. Each evening, dedicate five to ten minutes to write about your day, focusing on three questions: What went well? What challenges did I face? What will I do differently tomorrow? This exercise encourages mindful awareness of your actions and emotions. Research published in the Journal of Experimental Psychology indicates that daily reflective writing enhances emotional regulation and boosts self-efficacy, the belief in your ability to succeed. Over time, you'll notice patterns emerging, giving you clarity about your strengths and areas for improvement essential insight for effective self-coaching. Next, consider the **Wheel of Life** exercise. This visual tool helps you assess balance across key areas such as health, relationships, career, and personal growth. Draw a circle divided into segments representing these domains, then rate your satisfaction in each area on a scale of 1 to 10. Coaching studies show that visualizing balance increases motivation by revealing neglected areas and reinforcing commitment to holistic development. As your own coach, you can revisit the wheel periodically to adjust your focus and celebrate progress in neglected segments, preventing burnout and maintaining enthusiasm. Another practical method is the **ABC Model**, adapted from cognitive behavioral therapy but widely used in coaching. ABC stands for Activating event, Beliefs about the event, and Consequences (emotional and behavioral). When faced with a setback, map out these three elements to identify unhelpful beliefs that might be limiting your progress. For example, if you missed a workout (activating event), you might think, "I'm lazy" (belief), which leads to feelings of guilt and quitting (consequences). By recognizing this, you can reframe your beliefs with evidence-based alternatives like "I was tired today, but I can try again tomorrow," reducing negative self-talk and fostering resilience. Research confirms that reframing thoughts in this way significantly improves motivation and persistence. Goal visualization is another evidence-based self-coaching tool. Studies in sports psychology reveal that vividly imagining yourself achieving a goal activates the same brain regions as physical practice, boosting confidence and performance. As your own coach, spend a few minutes daily picturing successful outcomes whether acing a presentation, maintaining a new habit, or reaching a milestone. Visualization primes your brain for success and clarifies the steps needed to reach your goals. To deepen this practice, combine visualization with positive affirmations, statements that reinforce your capabilities, such as "I am focused and capable of achieving my goals." Affirmations, when consistent, can reshape neural pathways associated with self-esteem and reduce stress responses. To track progress effectively, adopt the **Progressive Tracking System (PTS)**, which involves breaking your goals into measurable weekly targets. Write down specific actions and assign daily or weekly deadlines. At the end of each week, review your accomplishments and obstacles. Research on goal progress tracking highlights the motivational impact of incremental feedback—small wins trigger dopamine release, reinforcing commitment. PTS turns overwhelming goals into manageable tasks, minimizing procrastination and encouraging steady advancement. Many productivity apps incorporate these principles, but even a handwritten planner works well. Develop a **Self-Coaching Ritual**, a consistent routine that signals your brain it's time for coaching. This might include meditation, deep breathing, and reviewing your journal and goals every morning or evening. Rituals anchor your self-coaching practice in your daily life and build discipline. Neuroscience shows that habits form through repeated contextual cues, so linking coaching activities with a fixed time and environment increases adherence and effectiveness.

Real-world coaching examples offer inspiration. Consider Serena Williams, who uses a mental coach to guide her focus and self-belief during high-pressure matches. While you may not have a personal coach, the techniques and tools outlined here let you embody that role yourself, harnessing your brain's capacity to learn, adapt, and thrive. Self-coaching is a skill that grows stronger with consistent practice— each tool adds a new layer of insight and motivation to propel you forward. One of the most powerful ways to learn self-coaching is by examining the lives of remarkable individuals who, despite challenges and limited external guidance, became their own greatest mentors. Their stories reveal how coaching psychology principles can be lived in everyday reality, providing a blueprint for anyone willing to take charge of their growth. These case studies highlight how self-coaching through reflection, resilience, goal-setting, and motivation translates into extraordinary achievements.

Consider **Elon Musk**, a global icon of innovation and entrepreneurship. Musk's journey epitomizes the self-coaching mindset. Though initially educated in physics and economics, he ventured into unfamiliar industries like aerospace and electric vehicles without traditional coaching or expert mentors in those fields. Instead, Musk has described a rigorous process of self-directed learning, where he breaks down complex problems into first principles, a method of reasoning that involves deconstructing ideas to their most fundamental truths. This approach aligns with coaching psychology's emphasis on reflective questioning and reframing limiting beliefs. Musk's ability to coach himself through failures like the early rocket crashes of SpaceX by learning, adjusting, and persisting has revolutionized entire industries. His story demonstrates how deep reflection, intellectual curiosity, and unwavering motivation are core self-coaching traits. Another inspiring figure is **Oprah Winfrey**, whose self-coaching journey began amidst adversity. Growing up in poverty and facing numerous personal challenges, Oprah developed a daily practice of self-reflection and goal visualization early in her career. She credits journaling as a pivotal tool in coaching herself through periods of doubt and fear. Oprah's deliberate focus on gratitude and aligning her work with her core values exemplifies the self-determination theory in coaching psychology, which says motivation thrives when actions connect with personal meaning. Her transformation from a troubled youth to a media powerhouse underscores the importance of emotional regulation, mindfulness, and accountability techniques that anyone can adopt when coaching themselves. In the sports world, **Michael Jordan** is often hailed as a self-coaching legend. Despite his natural talent, Jordan's success was rooted in relentless self-discipline and reflective practice. He famously used setbacks like being cut from his high school basketball team as motivation to intensify his training and improve his mental toughness. Jordan's routine included daily visualization exercises, imagining game-winning shots, which aligns with sports psychology's proven impact on performance. His career is a case study in using failure as feedback rather than defeat, a core coaching psychology concept. Jordan's habit of setting progressively challenging goals and tracking his improvements also mirrors modern self-coaching frameworks. From the arts, **Frida Kahlo** provides a unique example of self-coaching through creative resilience. Despite debilitating physical injuries and emotional pain, Kahlo cultivated an inner dialogue of strength and acceptance. Her art became a form of self-expression and emotional processing, a strategy parallel to journaling in coaching psychology. Kahlo's ability to reframe suffering as a source of inspiration reveals the power of cognitive reframing, helping maintain motivation even when external circumstances are bleak. Her life encourages anyone coaching themselves to embrace vulnerability as a tool for growth.

In Science and Invention, **Marie Curie** embodies self-coaching through curiosity and perseverance. Working in a male-dominated field with limited resources, Curie's disciplined study habits, meticulous goal-setting, and reflective practices allowed her to push boundaries in physics and chemistry. Curie's letters and diaries reveal a methodical approach to problem-solving and self-assessment, consistent with the GROW coaching model. Her story reminds us that self-coaching is not reserved for the elite, it's accessible to anyone willing to commit to lifelong learning and self-guidance.

These case studies, spanning entrepreneurship, media, sports, art, and science, share common threads: deliberate reflection, goal clarity, emotional resilience, and unwavering motivation. They show that coaching yourself is not a luxury but a necessity for turning challenges into stepping stones toward success. By studying their journeys, you can adopt proven self-coaching strategies tailored to your own path, fostering growth and transformation from within. Journaling is one of the most effective tools for self-coaching, transforming abstract thoughts into clear insights and fostering emotional intelligence. Yet, to truly harness its power, your journaling must go beyond mere recording of events. It needs to be intentional, reflective, and action-oriented. Begin your session by setting a **clear intention**. Ask yourself: "What do I want to learn or achieve today?" Setting an intention primes your brain to focus and aligns your actions with your bigger goals. Neuroscience research shows that intention-setting activates prefrontal cortex areas responsible for goal-directed behavior, improving attention and self-control.

Midday, perform a **mindfulness check-in**. Pause and take 3 deep breaths, then ask: "How am I feeling right now? What do I need?" Mindfulness practices improve emotional regulation and focus, essential qualities for effective self-coaching. In the evening, engage in a **self-compassion exercise**. Write a letter to yourself acknowledging your efforts and forgiving any mistakes made. Dr. Kristin Neff's research emphasizes that self-compassion reduces burnout and encourages persistence, making it a vital component of sustainable growth. While many self-coaching guides emphasize goal-setting, positive thinking, and time management, there are deeper, less commonly discussed techniques rooted in cutting-edge neuroscience and psychology that can revolutionize how you coach yourself. These rare insights aren't just theoretical. They have been quietly applied by high achievers, elite athletes, and top executives to unlock extraordinary performance. As your own coach, mastering these subtle yet powerful strategies will give you a distinctive edge on your journey. First, consider the concept of **"mental contrasting with implementation intentions" (MCII)**, a technique pioneered by psychologist Gabriele Oettingen. Unlike simple positive visualization, MCII combines imagining a desired future with a realistic assessment of obstacles and "if-then" planning. For example, instead of only visualizing success, you consciously identify what might block you (e.g., procrastination) and create a specific plan: "If I feel distracted, then I will immediately do a 2-minute breathing exercise." Research shows that MCII significantly improves goal attainment compared to positive thinking alone, because it integrates motivation with action readiness. This method remains underutilized in mainstream coaching but is a goldmine for self-coaching. Another rarely discussed technique is **"interoceptive awareness"**, the ability to sense internal bodily signals such as heartbeat, breathing, and gut feelings. Most people overlook this, yet emerging neuroscience research links interoceptive awareness to better emotional regulation, decision-making, and resilience. Elite performers often cultivate this subtle bodily awareness through practices like focused breathing and body scans. For self-coaching, becoming attuned to your physiological states allows you to detect early signs of stress or fatigue, enabling timely intervention before overwhelm takes hold. This deeper mind-body connection is foundational to sustainable motivation but is seldom explicitly taught. Closely related is the practice of **"prefrontal cortex priming."** Modern life bombards us with distractions that hijack this region. Rare self-coaching approaches emphasize deliberately priming this brain area before engaging in important tasks, through rituals such as "power posing," short mindfulness sessions, or controlled breathing techniques like box breathing. Research from Stanford University shows these micro-interventions increase cognitive control and reduce stress hormones. By training yourself to prepare your brain in this way, you maximize focus and decision-making—an insider's secret among elite CEOs and military leaders. A subtle but powerful mindset shift often hidden from public discourse is **embracing "productive discomfort."** Most self-help encourages comfort, yet growth hinges on tolerating and even seeking discomfort in a focused way. Psychologists differentiate between "distress" (unproductive pain) and "eustress" (positive stress that sharpens performance). Self-coaching at an advanced level involves training yourself to recognize discomfort as a signal of growth opportunity rather than threat. Techniques include brief exposure to challenging situations combined with reflective processing to build tolerance. This deliberate discomfort practice rewires your stress response to support resilience and creativity traits consistently observed in top performers across disciplines. A rarely emphasized but transformative self-coaching approach is **"meta-cognitive self-dialogue."** This is the art of stepping outside your own thoughts and observing your thinking patterns without judgment. While mindfulness touches on this, meta-cognition goes deeper, enabling you to recognize when your internal narrative drifts into sabotage, perfectionism, or procrastination, and consciously redirect it. Advanced self-coaches cultivate a "coach persona" within an internal voice that questions limiting beliefs and offers compassionate, constructive feedback. Neuroscience links meta-cognitive ability to higher emotional intelligence and adaptive decision-making, making it a pinnacle skill in self-guided growth. Incorporating these rarely shared, research-backed techniques into your self-coaching toolbox empowers you to transcend surface-level motivation and develop profound mental agility, emotional resilience, and sustained focus. These strategies are the hidden architecture behind the success of many top performers and thought leaders now within your reach as you coach yourself with intention and sophistication. Turning rare, research-backed self-coaching techniques into everyday habits requires clear, practical steps that anyone can follow, regardless of background or schedule.

1. Mental Contrasting with Implementation Intentions (MCII):

Start your day with a brief MCII session. Take 5 minutes to visualize a meaningful goal or outcome you want to achieve that day. Imagine the benefits and positive feelings as vividly as possible. Then, switch focus and realistically identify one or two obstacles that could hinder progress. Write them down. Next, create an "if-then" plan for each obstacle. For example, if your obstacle is "feeling distracted," your plan could be, "If I catch myself losing focus, then I will stand up and stretch for one minute." Research shows that specifying when and how to act primes your brain for immediate response, boosting self-control and follow-through.

2. Developing Interoceptive Awareness:

Set aside 3 to 5 minutes at least twice daily for focused body awareness exercises. Find a quiet spot and close your eyes. Slowly scan your body from head to toe, paying attention to sensations such as tension, warmth, or subtle movements of breath. To deepen this, try a breathing-focused practice: place one hand on your chest, one on your belly, and notice how your breath feels in different parts of your body. Tracking subtle changes in heart rate or digestion can be done by tuning in gently, without judgment.

This practice heightens your sensitivity to internal cues. Over time, you'll notice early signs of stress or fatigue, giving you an opportunity to apply calming techniques or take breaks before overwhelm occurs.

3. Prefrontal Cortex Priming Rituals:

Before starting important or challenging tasks, spend 2–3 minutes doing one of these rituals to "prime" your brain:

Power Posing: Stand or sit in an expansive posture (open chest, shoulders back) for 2 minutes. Research suggests this increases confidence and reduces cortisol, the stress hormone.

Box Breathing: Inhale for 4 seconds, hold for 4, exhale for 4, hold for 4, and repeat. This controlled breathing calms the nervous system and enhances focus.

Micro-Meditation: Close your eyes and focus on your breath or a calming word for 2 minutes.

Consistently practicing these rituals helps you enter a focused state with greater ease and resilience.

4. Embracing Productive Discomfort:

Begin by identifying a small, manageable discomfort you can expose yourself to daily. This could be speaking up in a meeting, tackling a difficult conversation, or sitting in silence without distractions for 5 minutes.

After the experience, journal briefly about how you felt before, during, and after. Reflect on whether the discomfort brought growth, new insight, or relief. Over time, gradually increase the difficulty or duration.

This practice trains your nervous system to tolerate stress positively and reframes discomfort as an ally rather than an enemy.

5. Meta-Cognitive Self-Dialogue:

Set a daily alarm or reminder to pause and observe your internal dialogue for 2 minutes. Ask yourself:

> "What am I thinking right now?" "Is this thought helping me or holding me back?"

Practice responding mentally with kindness and constructive feedback. Write down recurring sabotaging thoughts and challenge their validity. By cultivating this "coach within," you build emotional intelligence and the ability to self-correct without harsh judgment. Real-life stories bring abstract concepts to life, revealing how advanced self-coaching techniques translate into tangible, transformative change. Take, for example, Maya, a mid-level executive in a fast-paced tech company in Singapore. She struggled with chronic procrastination and self-doubt, which limited her ability to lead projects confidently. After learning about mental contrasting with implementation intentions (MCII), Maya began dedicating five minutes each morning to visualize her daily goals while realistically anticipating obstacles. She crafted specific "if-then" plans, such as "If I feel distracted during meetings, then I will jot down quick notes to regain focus." Within weeks, Maya noticed her productivity soared and her anxiety diminished. The MCII approach helped her harness motivation while remaining grounded, a balance she previously found elusive. Across the ocean, in Stockholm, Johan, an elite marathon runner, credits his breakthrough performance to cultivating interoceptive awareness. While many athletes focus purely on physical training, Johan incorporated twice-daily body scans and breathing exercises to tune into subtle signs of fatigue and stress. This heightened bodily awareness enabled him to adjust training intensity before injury or burnout set in. Researchers have shown that such interoceptive practices enhance emotional regulation and decision-making under pressure both critical for endurance sports. Johan's success story exemplifies how mind-body connection, often overlooked in self-coaching, becomes a competitive edge. In New York City, Sarah, a high-powered lawyer, struggled with decision fatigue and executive burnout. She began a simple yet effective prefrontal cortex priming ritual each morning: two minutes of box breathing followed by a power pose before entering the office. This brief practice shifted her physiological state from anxious and scattered to calm and focused, enabling sharper legal analysis and stronger client interactions. Neuroscience research supports how such rituals activate executive brain regions and reduce stress hormones, validating Sarah's experience. This subtle daily habit transformed her work performance and overall well-being. Meanwhile, in Cape Town, Thabo, an emerging social entrepreneur, embraced the concept of productive discomfort to grow his leadership skills. Initially terrified of public speaking, Thabo committed to intentionally exposing himself to small, uncomfortable situations starting with brief presentations at local community meetings. Journaling after each event, he reflected on how discomfort fueled growth rather than breakdown. Over time, Thabo's nervous system rewired to interpret stress as a challenge, not a threat. His increasing confidence helped him rally support for his ventures, proving how productive discomfort catalyzes resilience and creativity. Finally. In Tokyo,

Aiko, a creative director at an advertising agency, developed meta-cognitive self-dialogue as a tool to combat perfectionism and self-sabotage. Twice daily, she paused to observe her internal narrative, questioning thoughts that eroded her confidence. By cultivating a compassionate inner coach, Aiko learned to redirect negative self-talk toward encouragement and constructive feedback. This mental shift lifted a heavy burden of anxiety and unlocked creative flow, leading to innovative campaigns that garnered industry recognition. Meta-cognition, rarely highlighted in popular self-help, emerged as her secret weapon. Take the example of Priya, a young software engineer in Bengaluru. Like many in the high-pressure IT sector, she struggled with burnout and lack of focus. When she discovered the technique of mental contrasting with implementation intentions (MCII), Priya started each day by visualizing her work goals but also acknowledging likely distractions such as constant notifications or late-night fatigue. She formed specific "if-then" plans like, "If I get overwhelmed by emails, then I will take a five-minute walk." Over time, this practice helped Priya regain control over her attention and productivity, a breakthrough that deepened her confidence and reduced stress in her demanding job.

In the bustling city of Mumbai, Ramesh, a middle-aged small business owner running a textile shop, found his health declining under mounting pressures. Inspired by stories of holistic wellbeing, he began practicing interoceptive awareness through simple body scans and mindful breathing every morning before opening his store. Though initially unfamiliar with such concepts, Ramesh noticed how tuning into his body helped him detect early signs of fatigue and manage his blood pressure better. Indian research in integrative health confirms that combining traditional mindfulness with body awareness promotes emotional stability and resilience. For Ramesh, this mind-body connection became a vital tool for balancing work stress and family life. In Delhi, Anjali, a young lawyer navigating a competitive career, experienced decision fatigue and anxiety, common challenges in India's fast-paced legal field. She incorporated a brief prefrontal cortex priming ritual before court sessions, involving box breathing and standing in a confident posture. This small daily ritual, supported by neuroscience research, helped her calm nerves and sharpen mental clarity during high-stakes arguments. Anjali's journey reflects a growing awareness among Indian professionals that mental preparation rituals though rarely taught can significantly enhance focus and emotional regulation. In the rural district of Tamil Nadu, Arjun, an aspiring social worker, confronted his fear of public speaking and community engagement through the concept of productive discomfort. Starting with small group meetings in his village, he deliberately embraced moments of discomfort and reflected on them in a diary. His persistence rewired his relationship with stress, transforming anxiety into fuel for personal growth and leadership. This mirrors ancient Indian philosophies that value embracing challenges for spiritual and personal evolution, giving Arjun a culturally resonant framework for resilience. In Kolkata, Meera, a creative entrepreneur in the arts, struggled with perfectionism that hampered her progress. She adopted meta-cognitive self-dialogue by taking quiet moments throughout her day to observe and gently question her inner critical voice. Over time, Meera nurtured an internal "coach" who guided her with kindness and perspective. Neuroscience supports that this practice enhances emotional intelligence and creativity qualities increasingly recognized in India's evolving startup and arts scenes. Meera's transformation illustrates how self-awareness and self-compassion are powerful tools for unlocking potential, especially in India's culturally diverse and competitive environments. As you read these examples, imagine how integrating these techniques can transform your own life, helping you coach yourself with wisdom and sophistication few ever attain. In India today, where old traditions meet new technology, people are finding exciting ways to coach themselves using both ancient wisdom and modern science. Whether in busy cities or peaceful villages, Indians are learning how to understand their minds and bodies better to stay motivated and focused. Scientists and experts in India have studied these methods, proving that they really work and fit well with our way of life. One important skill is learning to notice what is happening inside your body, your heartbeat, your breathing, and how tense or relaxed your muscles are. This practice is very old in India because of yoga and meditation, but now science also shows that paying attention to these signs helps people control their emotions and stay calm under pressure. Many people in India, from office workers in Mumbai to farmers in Punjab, have found that tuning into their bodies helps them make better decisions and handle stress better. Another helpful technique is called "brain priming." It means doing small things to prepare your mind before a big task, like taking deep breaths or standing in a confident way. Research done in Indian universities shows that these simple actions can calm your nerves and sharpen your focus. For students preparing for exams or professionals getting ready for presentations, these quick mental warm-ups make a big difference. What's great is that these practices connect with Indian traditions, making them easier and more natural to do. India's rich culture also teaches us the value of facing challenges and discomfort to grow stronger. Many schools and community programs in India now encourage students and young people to step out of their comfort zones like speaking in front of others or trying new thingsand then reflect on their experiences. Studies show this helps build confidence and emotional strength. This idea fits well with Indian values of hard work and perseverance, motivating people to keep improving even when it feels hard.

Talking kindly to yourself is another powerful tool. Researchers in India have found that when people learn to notice negative thoughts but respond with kindness instead of criticism, their anxiety and sadness reduce. This practice of friendly inner dialogue is becoming part of therapy and coaching in India, mixing modern psychology with spiritual ideas like self-compassion that many Indians already believe in. This helps people become their own supportive coach, especially when life gets tough. India's ancient practices of Yoga, Ayurveda, and meditation are not just traditions of the past; they are powerful tools that many Indians use today to coach themselves toward better health and a stronger mind. These practices have been studied by scientists in India and around the world, proving their benefits for both body and mind. When combined with modern coaching techniques, they create a unique and effective way to support personal growth and motivation.

Yoga, for example, is much more than just physical exercise. It trains the mind to stay calm and focused, helping people develop self-awareness and emotional control. Research from Indian institutes shows that regular yoga practice lowers stress hormones and improves concentration. Many working professionals in India find that starting the day with simple yoga stretches and breathing exercises helps clear their minds and prepare them for the challenges ahead. This mental clarity is a key part of being your own coach, because it allows you to recognize when your mind is wandering or getting overwhelmed and gently bring it back to your goals.

Ayurveda, India's traditional system of medicine, teaches that balance in the body leads to balance in the mind. According to Ayurveda, each person has a unique constitution, or "dosha," that influences how they respond to stress and motivation. Research in Indian universities has begun to explore how Ayurvedic diets, herbal remedies, and daily routines support mental clarity and emotional well-being.

When you follow practices that fit your body type and lifestyle, you feel more energized and motivated. This personalized approach to health is a perfect example of coaching yourself by listening closely to your body's needs.

Meditation is another ancient tool that has become very popular in India and across the world. Scientific studies from Indian research centers confirm that meditation reduces anxiety, improves memory, and boosts creativity. Many Indians practice meditation as part of their daily routine not only to relax but also to develop a deeper connection with themselves. This self-connection is essential for self-coaching because it helps you observe your thoughts without judgment, allowing you to spot negative patterns and replace them with positive, encouraging ones. Meditation teaches patience and kindness toward yourself, qualities every good coach needs.

Together, Yoga, Ayurveda, and meditation create a strong foundation for self-coaching in India. They teach us to slow down, listen to our bodies and minds, and create habits that support long-term well-being. When these practices are combined with modern psychological techniques like goal setting, tracking progress, and managing motivation, they form a powerful toolkit. Indians from all walks of life

- students, homemakers, entrepreneurs are discovering how this blend helps them stay focused, motivated, and resilient. India's ancient wisdom holds a treasure trove of knowledge that has guided millions for thousands of years. Many of these old teachings offer profound tools for coaching yourself helping you stay motivated, focused, and balanced in the ups and downs of life. What is truly amazing is that modern research continues to uncover how these techniques affect the mind and body in ways that support personal growth and emotional strength.

One of the oldest Indian texts, the **Bhagavad Gita**, is essentially a masterclass in self-coaching. It teaches that true success comes not from external rewards but from mastering your own mind. The Gita encourages self-awareness, discipline, and focusing on your duties without attachment to results. This idea of "detached involvement" is powerful for today's world where distractions and pressures are everywhere. Studies on mindfulness, a concept closely related to the Gita's teachings, show how detachment helps reduce stress and improve focus. By applying these lessons daily, Indians learn to coach themselves calmly through challenges without losing hope or motivation. Another ancient Indian system, **Sankhya philosophy**, explains how our mind works through three qualities called "gunas": sattva (clarity), rajas (activity), and tamas (inertia). Understanding these gunas helps you recognize your current mental state and consciously move toward balance. For example, if you feel lazy or stuck (tamas), you can take steps to increase energy and clarity (rajas and sattva). Modern psychology supports this idea by emphasizing emotional awareness and regulation as keys to motivation and goal achievement. The gunas give a uniquely Indian lens on how to coach your emotions and energy throughout the day.

Pranayama, the ancient Indian science of breath control, is another self-coaching gem. Texts like the *Hatha Yoga Pradipika* describe various breathing techniques that calm the nervous system, reduce anxiety, and sharpen concentration. Indian scientists have studied pranayama extensively and confirmed that controlled breathing lowers heart rate and calms the mind, creating the perfect state for thoughtful decision-making and motivation. Practicing pranayama is like resetting your mental dashboard, giving you clear signals to guide your next move just like a good coach would. The concept of **Dharma**, one's personal duty or purpose is central to Indian philosophy and self-coaching. When you align your daily actions with your dharma, you find deeper meaning and motivation. Recent research from Indian universities shows that people who connect their work and goals to a higher purpose experience greater satisfaction and perseverance. This connection keeps the inner coach strong, pushing you forward even when external rewards are slow or uncertain. It reminds us that motivation is not just about quick wins, but about living a life true to who we are. India's ancient wisdom is not just a collection of techniques; it is deeply spiritual knowledge that understands the human being as an inseparable blend of mind, body, and soul. When you learn to coach yourself using these traditional Indian studies and methods, you are also stepping into a spiritual path, a journey toward self-realization and inner harmony, which strengthens your ability to face life's challenges with courage and clarity.

The practice of self-coaching in the Indian context cannot be separated from spirituality because the ancient texts teach us that true growth begins within. The **Bhagavad Gita**, one of India's most revered spiritual guides, explains that the mind is the battlefield where self-mastery happens. It urges us to observe our thoughts and emotions without attachment or fear, cultivating detachment alongside dedication. This teaching is at the heart of coaching yourself, the ability to remain calm amid struggles, to see beyond temporary failures, and to keep your focus on the higher purpose or "Dharma." This spiritual awareness transforms self-coaching from mere task management to a soulful process of aligning actions with your deeper values.

The understanding of the **gunas**, sattva, rajas, and tamasfrom Sankhya philosophy further connects self-coaching to spirituality. These qualities reflect the spiritual state of the mind: sattva represents clarity and purity; rajas, energy and movement; tamas, inertia and darkness. When you recognize which guna dominates your mind at any moment, you engage in a spiritual self-assessment. The goal is not just to "fix" yourself but to nurture sattva, the spiritual quality that brings peace, wisdom, and steady motivation. Thus, self-coaching becomes an act of spiritual purification—clearing mental fog and balancing energy to support your growth. Breath control, or **Pranayama**, is another beautiful example of how Indian self-coaching is intertwined with spirituality. Breath is seen as the bridge between the body and the spirit. Controlling the breath calms the nervous system, but beyond the physical benefits, it connects you to the life force or "Prana" flowing through you. This spiritual connection enhances your inner awareness and helps your inner coach become sensitive to your needs, guiding you gently rather than pushing harshly. Through pranayama, self-coaching becomes a sacred practice of tuning into your own rhythm and energy. The concept of **Dharma** often translated as duty or purpose is deeply spiritual and vital for self-coaching in India. Dharma reminds you that your life has a unique calling, and when your goals align with this calling, motivation naturally flows. Spiritually, Dharma connects you to a cosmic order; your efforts are not isolated struggles but part of a larger, meaningful tapestry. This understanding nurtures patience and persistence in self-coaching because it offers a sense of belonging and contribution beyond individual success. Self-coaching is not a one-time effort; it is a daily commitment to nurture yourself with awareness, purpose, and patience. Ancient Indian wisdom offers many simple yet profound routines that you can adopt each day to keep your inner coach active, motivated, and spiritually connected. These practices are designed not just to improve performance but to deepen your connection with yourself and the world around you, creating balance and peace in the process. Start your day with **early morning meditation** or silent reflection, often practiced by sages for thousands of years. In India, waking up before sunrise is considered an auspicious time called **Brahma Muhurta**. When the mind is naturally calm and receptive. Sitting quietly in this peaceful hour, focusing on your breath or repeating a simple mantra, tunes your mind toward clarity and calmness. This spiritual practice acts as a reset button for your inner coach, preparing you to face the day's challenges with a steady heart and clear mind. Scientific research supports early meditation's benefits for reducing anxiety and improving attention, confirming the wisdom of this ancient routine.

Next, consider **setting your intention** for the day aligned with your Dharma, or higher purpose. In Indian tradition, this is like offering a prayer or dedication to your actions, reminding yourself why you do what you do. This intention-setting keeps your motivation rooted in meaning, not just in completing tasks or chasing rewards. When your actions reflect a greater purpose, your inner coach stays inspired and focused. Modern psychology echoes this by showing that people who link their daily goals to personal values are more resilient and engaged.

Throughout the day, integrate the practice of **mindful breath awareness**. Taking brief pauses to observe your breathing whether in traffic, before a meeting, or during a stressful moment helps calm your nervous system and refocus your mind. This simple pranayama-inspired habit reconnects you to your spiritual center, allowing your inner coach to guide you gently rather than with force. Studies in India and worldwide show that such breathing breaks reduce cortisol levels (the stress hormone) and enhance decision-making under pressure. Another powerful routine is **gratitude journaling**, adapted from ancient Indian practices of daily reflection. Each evening, write down three things you are grateful for this could be people, experiences, or personal qualities. Gratitude nurtures sattva, the guna associated with peace and clarity, which supports motivation and wellbeing. Spiritually, gratitude connects you to abundance rather than lack, shifting your inner dialogue from criticism to appreciation. Indian research in positive psychology has confirmed that regular gratitude practice improves emotional resilience and happiness, reinforcing its value as a self-coaching tool.

To track your progress spiritually, consider the ancient Indian practice of **Svadhyaya** which is self-study. This means observing not only your external achievements but your inner growth, thoughts, and emotional responses. Journaling can include reflections on what lessons a setback taught you, how your patience was tested, or where you felt alignment with your higher self. This honest self-observation is not for self-judgment but for compassionate learning, turning every experience into a step forward on your spiritual and coaching journey.

End your day with a **short ritual of surrender and gratitude**, such as lighting a candle or offering a quiet prayer of thanks for the day's lessons. This ritual honors the idea that while you work hard, there is a bigger cosmic order supporting you. Letting go of control at night helps your mind rest deeply and prepares your inner coach for the next day with renewed energy and faith. When we talk about coaching ourselves, the wisdom of ancient Indian heroes shines as timeless guidance. These figures, often celebrated in scriptures, epics, and folklore, were not just warriors or kings. They were masters of their minds and spirits, showing how self-coaching rooted in spirituality can lead to greatness beyond the battlefield or throne. Their stories offer us powerful lessons on resilience, inner strength, and purposeful action, all essential qualities for anyone striving to be their own coach today. Take **Arjuna**, the legendary warrior of the Mahabharata, who faced a crisis of confidence on the battlefield of Kurukshetra. His inner turmoil and doubt mirror the struggles we all face when motivation fades or fear creeps in. What saved Arjuna was the guidance of his spiritual coach, Lord Krishna, who revealed profound truths about duty, self-control, and detachment in the Bhagavad Gita. Krishna's teachings encouraged Arjuna to rise above his fears and focus on his Dharma, his righteous path. Spiritually, this dialogue emphasizes that coaching oneself means recognizing the divine wisdom within, detaching from outcomes, and acting with integrity. Arjuna's transformation teaches us that self-coaching is also about cultivating faith in a higher purpose and finding courage in clarity.

Another inspiring figure is **Chanakya**, the ancient political strategist and philosopher who shaped the foundation of Indian governance and economics. Known for his sharp intellect and unyielding discipline, Chanakya practiced rigorous self-discipline and introspection, applying methods that resemble modern coaching tools like goal setting, self-monitoring, and strategic planning. His famous work, the *Arthashastra*, is full of practical advice on leadership and personal conduct, but underlying it all is a deep spiritual awareness of balance, ethics, and duty. Chanakya's life shows us how self-coaching can be both strategic and grounded in values, combining mental clarity with moral strength. **Rani Lakshmibai of Jhansi**, the fearless queen who fought bravely during India's First War of Independence, is another powerful example. Beyond her courage on the battlefield, she embodied self-coaching through unwavering determination, resilience, and inner strength. Historical accounts tell us how she balanced the fierce demands of war with moments of deep prayer and meditation, drawing spiritual energy to sustain her resolve. Her ability to inspire and lead herself in the darkest hours reflects a spiritual self-coaching that integrates action with faith and emotional control. For modern self-coachers, her story is a reminder that inner spiritual resilience fuels outer achievements.

The yogic sage **Patanjali**, credited with compiling the *Yoga Sutras*, also provides a profound blueprint for self-coaching. His system teaches that the mind's fluctuations cause suffering, and by steadying these fluctuations through ethical living, meditation, and self-discipline, one can achieve clarity and peace. Patanjali's *Ashtanga Yoga* (Eight Limbs) is essentially a detailed self-coaching manual, guiding practitioners to cultivate self-awareness, discipline, and detachment. This spiritual path encourages self-coaching not as external pushing but as a gentle unfolding of your true potential through inner harmony.

Consider the example of our very own **Swami Vivekananda**, who revived ancient Indian spirituality in the modern era. His teachings on self-confidence, self-control, and relentless pursuit of one's mission echo the principles of coaching psychology. Vivekananda emphasized the power of the mind, stating, "You are what your thoughts have made you." His spiritual practice combined rigorous discipline with boundless faith in human potential, inspiring millions to become their own guides and leaders in life. His life demonstrates how ancient spiritual coaching techniques remain deeply relevant, motivating us to take charge of our destiny with courage and wisdom. The inspiring lives of ancient Indian heroes are not just stories from the past. They are living lessons that can shape how you coach yourself today. Their journeys reveal spiritual principles that, when translated into daily habits, can help you build resilience, clarity, and unwavering motivation. The secret lies in blending their inner wisdom with practical action, creating a daily self-coaching routine grounded in ancient Indian values.

One key lesson from heroes like Arjuna and Rani Lakshmibai is **courageous focus on Dharma**, or your life's purpose. Begin each day by reminding yourself of your personal "Dharma". Your true calling or the role you want to fulfill. This might be as simple as caring for your family, advancing your career with integrity, or serving your community. Write down your daily intention reflecting this higher purpose.

This habit helps your inner coach stay connected to meaning, not just busywork. In Indian spirituality, this alignment of action with Dharma strengthens mental clarity and brings peace, much like how Arjuna overcame his fears by focusing on his duty rather than the outcome.

Another practical habit inspired by Chanakya's discipline is **structured goal setting with ethical reflection**. Set clear, manageable goals for the day or week, but add a moment to reflect on whether these goals align with your values and the greater good. This reflection helps prevent burnout and keeps your motivation pure. For example, if you face a tough choice, ask yourself: "Is this action honest? Does it benefit others as well as me?" This practice echoes the ancient emphasis on righteousness (Dharma) and keeps your inner coach wise and compassionate, not merely driven by results.

Daily **mindfulness through breath and presence**, inspired by yogic sages like Patanjali, is another powerful habit. Take several short pauses during your day to observe your breath and center your awareness. Even a minute or two of deep, slow breathing calms your mind and reconnects you to your inner coach. This simple habit helps you stay grounded in the present, avoiding anxiety about past mistakes or future worries. When you act from this calm center, decisions become clearer, and motivation renews naturally. Modern science confirms the power of breath awareness to reduce stress and improve focus, aligning perfectly with ancient wisdom.

The ancient heroes also teach us the power of **resilience through spiritual surrender**. At the end of each day, spend a few minutes reflecting on what went well and what challenges you faced, then practice letting go of worries with a short prayer, affirmation, or silent gratitude. This habit mirrors Rani Lakshmibai's blend of fierce action and deep prayer, helping you rest peacefully and recharge your inner coach. Spiritual surrender is not giving up; it is trusting that your sincere efforts, combined with cosmic order, will bring growth in time. This mindset prevents the inner coach from becoming overly critical or anxious.

Lastly, cultivate **self-compassion as taught by Swami Vivekananda's teachings on self-love and confidence**. When you make mistakes or encounter setbacks, speak kindly to yourself as you would to a friend or mentor. Remind yourself that setbacks are part of the growth process. This daily practice of gentleness supports your inner coach in maintaining motivation and perseverance. Ancient Indian spirituality encourages seeing the divine spark in oneself, which fosters unconditional self-acceptance and courage. In the journey of becoming your own coach, incorporating spiritual exercises rooted in Indian traditions can deeply enhance your motivation and self-awareness. These exercises, practiced by sages and seekers for centuries, offer simple yet powerful ways to align your mind, body, and spirit, making your self-coaching practice holistic and sustainable.

One of the most effective exercises is **Japa meditation**, the repetition of a mantra or sacred phrase. Traditionally, this involves softly chanting a word or phrase like "Om" or "So Hum," but you can choose any positive phrase that resonates with you. The power of Japa lies in its ability to calm the restless mind and anchor your attention. For self-coaching, this practice helps you cultivate focus and inner calm, making it easier to listen to your inner guidance without distraction. Research on meditation shows that repetitive mantra chanting activates areas of the brain linked to attention and emotional regulation, echoing the ancient insight that sound and vibration can transform the mind.

Another transformative practice is **Pranayama**, or controlled breathing. Techniques like slow, deep breathing or alternate nostril breathing (Nadi Shodhana) help balance the nervous system and clear mental fog. This simple breathing exercise is accessible anytime you feel overwhelmed or unfocused. By consciously controlling your breath, you signal to your inner coach to slow down, observe, and respond wisely rather than react impulsively. Studies have demonstrated that pranayama reduces stress hormones and enhances cognitive function, confirming its value in modern self-coaching.

The ancient ritual of **Sandhya Vandana**, or daily prayers at dawn and dusk, teaches the importance of ritual and rhythm in self-coaching. These moments of quiet reflection offer a natural pause to review your intentions, express gratitude, and renew commitment to your goals. Creating your own mini-rituals, lighting a candle, sitting silently with folded hands, or writing a short note of thanks can connect you to the sacred dimension of your efforts. Rituals cultivate discipline and meaning, reinforcing your motivation with a spiritual foundation.

Another powerful tool is the practice of **Swadhyaya**, or self-study. This means honestly observing your thoughts, behaviors, and emotional patterns without judgment. Keeping a journal focused on self-reflection allows you to identify recurring blocks, triggers, and progress. Swadhyaya encourages curiosity rather than criticism, helping your inner coach understand your unique patterns and gently guide change. Indian spiritual teachers have long emphasized that self-knowledge is the key to liberation, and modern psychology confirms that self-reflection boosts emotional intelligence and resilience.

Finally, consider adopting **Seva**, or selfless service, as part of your coaching practice. Giving time or effort to help others, without expecting anything in return, cultivates humility, purpose, and joy. This outward expression of spirituality enriches your inner coach by reminding you that growth is not only personal but also relational. Serving others can boost your mood, reduce stress, and enhance feelings of connectedness is the key ingredients for sustained motivation and well-being. A unique and powerful framework from ancient Indian philosophy that can transform your self-coaching journey is the understanding of the *gunas*, the three fundamental qualities that influence everything in nature, including our mind and behavior. These are *Sattva* (purity, harmony, clarity), *Rajas* (activity, passion, restlessness), and *Tamas* (inertia, dullness, confusion). Knowing how these qualities operate within you offers deep insight into your motivation, mood, and decision-making, allowing you to customize your self-coaching approach for lasting balance.

Sattva represents the quality of clarity, wisdom, and calmness. When your mind is in a sattvic state, you feel motivated by joy, peace, and clear purpose. Tasks seem effortless, and your focus sharpens naturally. This is the ideal state for your inner coach to operate from because your decisions come from a place of harmony and self-awareness. For example, during periods of calm reflection or meditation, you tap into sattva energy, which helps you set meaningful goals aligned with your true values. Cultivating sattva can be as simple as spending time in nature, eating fresh and nourishing foods, or practicing gratitude habits known to uplift mood and clarity.

On the other hand, *Rajas* is the dynamic, restless energy that drives ambition and action. While rajas can propel you forward with enthusiasm and creativity, it can also create stress, impatience, and distraction if left unchecked. This is when your inner coach needs to gently remind you to slow down and focus. Recognizing when rajas dominates allows you to take conscious breaks or adopt calming spiritual exercises like pranayama or mantra meditation to regain balance. For instance, many successful leaders and warriors from Indian history like Maharana Pratap or Shivaji Maharaj channeled rajas energy into disciplined action, yet knew when to retreat and regroup, embodying mastery over this force.

Tamas, the quality of inertia and confusion, often feels like a heavy fog of procrastination or negativity. When tamas rises, motivation dwindles, and you may struggle with self-doubt or lethargy. This is the most challenging state for your inner coach, but also the most important one to recognize. Ancient Indian wisdom suggests combating tamas by increasing light—both literally by exposing yourself to sunlight and metaphorically by engaging in uplifting activities, learning new things, or practicing chanting and physical activity. Even a short walk or mindful breathing can reduce tamas, shifting your mind toward sattva or rajas, thus restoring motivation.

The interplay of these three gunas is constantly shifting within you. The key to effective self-coaching is learning to observe which guna is dominant at any moment without judgment. This awareness creates a powerful meta-coaching skill knowing when to push forward, when to pause, and when to nurture yourself gently. For example, if you notice lethargy creeping in (tamas), your coach-self can decide to break tasks into smaller steps or take restorative rest. If impatience arises (rajas), you might choose to meditate or journal to calm your mind. When clarity and calmness (sattva) emerge, capitalize on this energy to tackle important challenges or reflect deeply.

Modern research in psychology parallels this ancient insight, showing how mood states and personality traits influence motivation and performance. Understanding your mental "climate" and adapting strategies accordingly leads to more sustainable growth than blindly pushing through resistance. This nuanced approach to self-coaching, rooted in Indian philosophy, empowers you to work with your nature rather than against it. To coach yourself effectively using the ancient wisdom of the *gunas*, the first essential step is learning to recognize which guna between *Sattva*, *Rajas*, or *Tamas* is currently influencing your thoughts, emotions, and behaviors. This self-awareness forms the foundation for making conscious shifts that enhance your motivation, clarity, and balance.

You can begin by observing your daily experiences without judgment. When your mind feels calm, clear, and joyful even amidst challenges. *Sattva* is likely dominant. You might notice a natural enthusiasm for learning, a sense of inner peace, or steady concentration. Physically, your body feels light and energized, your sleep is restful, and you crave wholesome, fresh foods. Mentally, you may be patient and compassionate, able to see situations from a wider perspective. For instance, a teacher in rural India who calmly inspires students despite hardships may be embodying sattvic qualities.

If instead, you notice restless energy, impatience, or a strong desire to act, create, or change your surroundings, *Rajas* is likely active. This guna fuels ambition and drive but can also bring anxiety, irritability, or frustration when results don't come quickly. You may feel physically tense, prone to interrupted sleep, or crave spicy, stimulating foods. An entrepreneur working long hours with bursts of intense focus and occasional frustration is experiencing rajasic energy. While useful for progress, unchecked rajas can exhaust you or cloud judgment.

When lethargy, confusion, or procrastination sets in, *Tamas* is influencing your state. You might feel mentally foggy, emotionally low, and physically heavy or tired. It's harder to get started on tasks, and you may crave heavy, oily, or processed foods. This state often accompanies feelings of discouragement or negativity. For example, a student overwhelmed by exam stress who avoids studying and feels stuck might be trapped in tamas.

Once you identify your predominant guna, the next step is learning how to shift consciously to a more balanced and productive state. Here are practical, spiritually grounded strategies for each shift:

From Tamas to Rajas or Sattva: Start with gentle physical movement such as stretching or walking outside in sunlight. The ancient Indian practice of *Surya Namaskar* (sun salutations) or simply sitting in natural light can help awaken your energy. Engage your breath deeply with a few rounds of slow pranayama to clear mental fog. Listen to uplifting music or chant a simple mantra to stimulate positive vibration. Avoid heavy meals or excessive rest, which deepen tamas. Journaling about one small positive goal for the day encourages mental movement.

From Rajas to Sattva: When you feel restless or overwhelmed, pause and slow your breath. Practice mindful breathing or meditation to calm mental turbulence. Incorporate moments of gratitude and self-compassion to ease harsh self-criticism. Engage in quiet reflection, perhaps sitting silently with folded hands and focusing on your intention or dharma. Avoid stimulants like caffeine or harsh criticism, which intensify rajas. Drinking warm herbal tea or spending time in a quiet, uncluttered space supports this calming shift.

Maintaining Sattva: To sustain sattva, cultivate daily rituals that honor balance like the balanced diet, regular meditation, meaningful work, and time in nature. Foster positive relationships and avoid gossip or negativity that feed tamas or rajas. Reflect on your progress with gentle curiosity, celebrating small wins to keep motivation steady. Study inspiring texts or stories of Indian heroes who embodied sattva, such as Swami Vivekananda, to deepen your spiritual connection.

The ancient sages emphasized that these shifts are not about perfection but about gentle awareness and flexibility. Like a gardener tending plants, your inner coach nurtures the mind's environment to support growth and harmony. This cycle of observing, shifting, and balancing your guna creates a dynamic coaching process rooted in deep spiritual wisdom and practical action.

Incorporating this ancient understanding into your daily self-coaching allows you to respond skillfully to life's ups and downs, transforming challenges into opportunities for growth. In Indian philosophy, the concept of *Swadharma*, meaning one's own duty or path holds profound wisdom for anyone striving to be their own coach. *Swadharma* teaches us that true motivation and fulfillment come not from imitating others or chasing external rewards but from understanding and living according to your unique purpose and nature. When your self-coaching aligns with your *Swadharma*, your actions gain deeper meaning, and your motivation becomes sustainable, rooted in authenticity rather than fleeting desires.

The Bhagavad Gita, a timeless spiritual text, beautifully explains the importance of following one's *Swadharma*. It urges individuals to perform their duties with dedication, even if imperfectly, rather than adopting someone else's path perfectly. This insight encourages self-acceptance and reduces inner conflict, two critical ingredients for effective self-coaching. When you accept your personal strengths, limitations, and passions without harsh judgment, your inner coach can guide you with compassion rather than pressure. Living in tune with *Swadharma* means beginning with self-discovery. What are the activities that make you feel alive, focused, and purposeful? What talents and values do you hold dear? What does your heart naturally pull you toward, even if it is challenging or unconventional? By exploring these questions honestly, you start building a coaching practice that respects your individuality, rather than trying to fit into generic templates of success.

A remarkable example from Indian history is the life of Dr. A.P.J. Abdul Kalam, the "Missile Man of India." Dr. Kalam's *Swadharma* was to serve his country through science and education, and his self-coaching focused on nurturing curiosity, discipline, and humility aligned with this purpose. Despite numerous obstacles, his inner coach remained committed to his path, motivating him to persevere. His life illustrates how embracing *Swadharma* fuels a deep, unwavering motivation that transcends external circumstances. In practical terms, incorporating *Swadharma* into self-coaching requires regular reflection and honest check-ins. Set aside moments to ask yourself: Are the goals I pursue aligned with my true interests and values? Am I motivated by external pressure, or does this work inspire me? Are my efforts sustainable and nourishing to my spirit? These reflections help avoid burnout and disillusionment, common traps when people chase goals disconnected from their essence.

Furthermore, *Swadharma* invites you to approach obstacles and failures with a new perspective. Instead of seeing setbacks as signs of personal inadequacy, view them as lessons that refine your understanding of your true path. This shift nurtures resilience and patience, empowering your inner coach to adapt strategies without losing sight of your core purpose.

Indian spiritual traditions also emphasize that *Swadharma* is not static but evolves with your growth and life circumstances. What feels like your duty today may transform as you gain new insights or enter new phases of life. Your self-coaching practice benefits from this fluidity, encouraging flexibility and openness rather than rigid expectations. Ultimately, when your self-coaching is grounded in *Swadharma*, motivation becomes less about pushing yourself and more about inviting your deepest self to emerge. It turns coaching into a sacred dialogue between your mind, heart, and spirit guided by timeless wisdom and personal authenticity. This holistic integration enriches every step of your journey, making your inner coach not just a motivator but a compassionate companion on the path to fulfillment. One of the most profound teachings from Indian spirituality that can transform your self-coaching practice is *Karma Yoga*, or the yoga of mindful, selfless action. This ancient path emphasizes doing your work with full attention and dedication, while letting go of attachment to the results. Integrating *Karma Yoga* into your self-coaching can help you sustain motivation and inner peace, even amid uncertainty and challenge.

In everyday terms, *Karma Yoga* encourages you to focus completely on the present moment and the task at hand, rather than being distracted by worries about the future or regrets from the past. When you practice mindful action, your energy flows more naturally, reducing mental fatigue and increasing productivity. This presence fosters a deep connection between effort and outcome, helping you develop trust in the process itself, not just the end result.

Ancient Indian sages taught that attachment to outcomes - success, failure, praise, or blame often leads to stress, anxiety, and burnout. Instead, *Karma Yoga* invites you to act with sincerity and discipline, while surrendering the fruits of your labor to a higher power or universal flow. This does not mean passivity or lack of ambition but rather a balanced mindset where effort and detachment coexist. Such a mindset frees your inner coach from harsh self-judgment, making motivation sustainable over the long term. This principle has practical value in self-coaching. For example, when you set goals, you naturally want to achieve them. But if you obsess over each result or compare yourself to others, your motivation may weaken, especially if progress feels slow. Applying *Karma Yoga*, you learn to celebrate each small effort and improvement, regardless of external validation. This acceptance nurtures resilience, as you become less shaken by setbacks and more focused on continual growth. Another key aspect of *Karma Yoga* is cultivating discipline through routine. Consistent daily practice whether in work, study, or self-care builds momentum and inner strength. This regularity anchors your motivation and prevents burnout caused by sporadic effort or overwhelming goals. Spiritual disciplines such as chanting, meditation, or simple breathing exercises support this consistency by centering the mind and calming distractions. Importantly, **Karma Yoga** aligns well with scientific findings about motivation and mental well-being. Studies in psychology show that mindfulness practices improve focus, reduce stress, and enhance emotional regulation. Likewise, people who adopt process-oriented goals, valuing effort and learning over fixed outcomes tend to sustain motivation longer and recover more easily from failure.

Incorporating *Karma Yoga* into your self-coaching creates a compassionate, empowering cycle: you act fully in the present, detach from excessive worry about results, and gently redirect your attention back whenever it wanders. This transforms motivation from a fragile flame into a steady light that guides you through both easy and difficult times. In India's old spiritual teachings, there is a special practice called *Swadhyaya*. It means looking inside yourself carefully and honestly to understand your thoughts, feelings, and actions. This is one of the best tools you can use to coach yourself. When you learn to reflect on yourself kindly, it helps you stay motivated and grow in a healthy way.

Swadhyaya is more than just thinking about things. It is about having a heart-to-heart talk with yourself. You ask questions like: "Who am I really? Why do I do what I do? Are my actions helping me reach my true goals?" These questions help you find out if there are hidden fears or bad habits stopping you from moving forward. Once you see these clearly, you can slowly change them. Ancient Indian teachers, like Patanjali, included *Swadhyaya* as an important part of yoga because they knew it cleans the mind and opens the way to wisdom. The Bhagavad Gita also tells us that knowing ourselves is the key to peace and right action. Even today, this idea is very useful if you want to be your own coach. You can practice *Swadhyaya* every day in simple ways. For example, keep a journal and write down your thoughts and feelings. This helps you notice patterns and understand yourself better over time. You can also try quiet meditation where you watch your thoughts without getting caught up in them. This helps calm your mind and stops the inner voice that often criticizes and lowers your motivation. A great example is Rukmini Devi Arundale, a famous Indian dancer and teacher. She said that looking inside herself regularly helped her stay motivated for many years, even when things were tough. She kept adjusting her efforts while staying true to her passion. Self-reflection also makes you more responsible for your own progress. When you check in with yourself daily and celebrate small wins, you feel more encouraged to keep going. This is much better than being harsh on yourself or ignoring what you have achieved. *Swadhyaya* also helps you listen to your inner guidance. Indian wisdom says inside every person there is a quiet inner guide, often called the *Antaryami*. When you take time to reflect, you get closer to this voice, which helps you make decisions that really fit your true self, instead of just following what others say.

Modern science agrees with this too. Studies show people who reflect on themselves often have better control of their emotions, set clearer goals, and feel more motivated from inside. This shows how Indian spiritual ideas and modern psychology support each other. Remember, self-reflection is not a one-time thing. Life changes, and so do you. That's why it's important to keep looking inside yourself regularly. This way, your self-coaching stays fresh, and you don't get stuck or tired.

In short, *Swadhyaya* makes you a better coach for yourself. It helps you understand who you are, be kind to yourself, and find real motivation that comes from within. With this practice, your inner coach becomes a wise friend who helps you move forward with confidence and peace.

7. The Unseen Teachers

Everyone wants success, but no one prays for pain. We run from failure, hide our tears, and curse the slow ticking of time when things don't go our way. But what if the very things we try hardest to avoid - pain, failure, and time are actually the greatest teachers life offers? Pain has a strange power. It strips away what doesn't matter and shows us what truly does. It quiets the noise of the world and forces us to listen to our soul. Think of the heartbreak that made you stronger. Or the rejection that led you down a better path. In those moments, we rarely say, "This is teaching me something." But years later, when we look back, the lessons are often written in bold.

Consider Thomas Edison. Before he invented the light bulb, he failed over 1,000 times. When a reporter asked him how it felt to fail so many times, Edison replied, "I didn't fail 1,000 times. The light bulb was an invention with 1,000 steps." That's the kind of perspective pain can give, if you let it. Pain doesn't mean you're broken. It means you're being reshaped. Failure is one of life's greatest illusions. Society teaches us that success is about always winning, always achieving, always being perfect. But real growth happens in the shadows of defeat. Scientific studies back this up. Let's take once again a real-life example of J.K. Rowling, the author of the Harry Potter series, was a single mother on welfare when she wrote her first book. She was rejected by 12 publishers before one said yes. Today, her books have sold over 500 million copies. Would she have become that resilient, that creative, without going through that phase of rejection and failure? Failure clears the way for reinvention. It humbles us, makes us rethink our methods, and forces us to reconnect with our deeper why. Sometimes, failure is not life punishing you, it's life redirecting you. Time is often misunderstood. We either rush it or resent it. But few realize that **time is not just a healer, it's also a revealer.** It heals our wounds, yes, but it also shows us truths we weren't ready to see before. Imagine a wound on your skin. No matter how much you want it to heal overnight, it won't. The body needs time and so does the heart, the mind, and the soul. But time doesn't just help us recover. It gives us perspective. Have you ever looked back on something you once cried over... and smiled? That's time showing you that **what once felt like the end was actually a beginning.** The storm that once scared you becomes the story that shapes you. We all go to school, read books, and take courses. But life teaches its deepest lessons in silence through **loss, heartbreak, uncertainty, and waiting.** This hidden curriculum is not found in textbooks. It's taught by invisible teachers:

Pain teaches us empathy.

Failure teaches us humility.

Time teaches us patience.

These three forces are often seen as enemies. But in reality, they are the very ingredients of greatness. Let's take the story of **Nelson Mandela**. He spent 27 years in prison. Most would break. But Mandela used that time to reflect, to grow, and to prepare himself to lead. When he was finally released, he didn't come out bitter. He came out better. He became a global symbol of peace and forgiveness.

His prison wasn't the end of his life . It was the classroom where he became who he was meant to be. There is a special kind of power in transforming our own pain into a guiding light for others. Imagine yourself standing in darkness, heart heavy with yesterday's wounds, and then choosing to carry a single flame forward. That small flame like your story illuminates a path not only for you but for anyone stumbling in similar shadows. This alchemy of suffering into service, of bruise into blessing, is at the heart of becoming the light for others.

Decades of psychological research confirm what countless spiritual traditions have long taught: posttraumatic growth is real. A landmark 2016 meta-analysis in the *Journal of Traumatic Stress* showed that nearly 50% of people who endure life's hardest blows report positive transformation, often driven by the desire to help others avoid the same pitfalls. When we share our scars, we offer a map through the territory of pain, and in doing so, we find healing ourselves. Consider the science of **empathetic resonance**, where our brains literally mirror the emotions of those around us. Functional MRI studies reveal that when we witness suffering, regions such as the anterior insula and anterior cingulate cortex activate areas linked to our own pain experiences. But here's the miracle: when we act with kindness, helping someone in distress, those same neural circuits light up with relief and reward. In this way, your act of compassion becomes a two-way bridge: you ease someone's burden and simultaneously bathe your own heart in light. In India, the ancient practice of **Seva**, the selfless service is both spiritual discipline and communal lifeline. From the gurudwaras offering langar (free meal) to the village well maintained by volunteers, Seva reminds us that serving another is serving the divine spark within ourselves. Modern studies from India's Tata Institute of Social Sciences found that individuals who engage in regular Seva report a 30% decrease in anxiety and a 25% boost in life satisfaction compared to those who serve less often. Such findings underscore a simple truth: when we give, we grow.

But service need not be grand to be profound. A gentle word in a moment of loneliness, a listening ear when someone feels unseen, a text that says, "I'm here for you" these small stones create ripples far beyond our sight. Research by Dr. Sonja Lyubomirsky at the University of California shows that even brief acts of kindness release oxytocin and endorphins, bolstering both giver and receiver. In real terms, offering a smile at a bus stop or a comforting message to a stressed friend can spark a self-perpetuating cycle of hope that echoes through families, workplaces, and communities. There is something magical about being truly heard. Think back to a time when you were hurting not just physically, but emotionally. Maybe you felt broken, lost, or completely invisible. And then someone sat beside you. They didn't try to fix you. They didn't interrupt. They didn't judge. They just... listened. That moment, even if silent, might have felt like a warm blanket in the cold. It may not have solved everything, but you probably felt less alone. That's the kind of power we all carry, the power to help someone heal, just by listening. Many people think helping others means giving advice or having all the answers. But often, the deepest healing comes from simply holding space for someone being there, fully present. In fact, a study published in the *Journal of Applied Psychology* showed that people who feel listened to deeply are more likely to overcome emotional pain, rebuild self-worth, and even improve their physical health over time. Listening is more than keeping quiet while someone speaks. It means putting away your phone, making eye contact, and truly caring about what they are saying. It's about being there not just with your ears, but with your heart. Psychologists call this **active listening**, and it's one of the most powerful tools we have for connection. When we truly listen to someone, we become a mirror for their emotions. They see themselves in our eyes, and something within them begins to settle. They feel safe, accepted, and validated. That's when real transformation begins, not with a grand speech, but with quiet presence. Let me tell you a personal story. Years ago, I was struggling with something I couldn't even put into words. My thoughts were heavy, my heart even heavier. One day, I sat with a friend and tried to explain what I was feeling. But I broke down. I expected them to get uncomfortable, to say, "Don't cry," or to change the topic. But they didn't. They just stayed with me, gently nodding, saying nothing only listening.

That moment didn't erase my pain, but it gave me strength. I felt seen. And from that day, I promised myself: whenever I see someone hurting, I will do for them what my friend did for me. I will be a safe place. This is how we become the light for others. Not by doing big things. But by showing up, again and again, with love, patience, and openness. You don't need training to be a healer. You just need to care deeply and listen with your whole being. In ancient Indian tradition, the idea of **"shravan"**, the act of sacred listening was considered a spiritual practice. The sages believed that when you listen deeply, without ego, you become a vessel for divine understanding. You don't just hear the words you hear the soul behind them. Imagine if each of us practiced this form of listening every day - in our homes, schools, workplaces, even with strangers. How many hearts would soften? How many people would feel lighter, just knowing someone truly hears them? Or how listening to someone else's struggle makes you feel less alone in your own? That is the quiet magic of storytelling. It heals not just the one who listens, but also the one who speaks.

In ancient India, storytelling wasn't just entertainment. It was wisdom, therapy, and spiritual transmission. From the *Panchatantra* to the *Mahabharata*, stories passed down lessons of courage, resilience, and self-realization. These weren't just fables, they were mirrors of human life, showing how people rise even after the darkest of times. Modern psychology now confirms what our ancestors knew. Telling your story, especially after trauma or pain, helps you process emotions and rebuild your identity. But there's something even more powerful: when you tell your story to help someone else. That's when your pain becomes medicine. I remember once speaking to a group of young students. I shared a story about a time in my life when I felt like a complete failure — overwhelmed, lost, and hopeless. It wasn't easy to talk about. But after the session, a shy boy came up to me, eyes filled with tears. "I thought I was the only one," he said. "But now I know I'm not broken. I'm just human." That moment reminded me — we don't have to be perfect to inspire others. We just have to be honest. Your story with all its cracks, heartbreaks, and mistakes has the power to reach someone's heart. It might help someone see light when all they see is darkness. It might give them the courage to keep going one more day. And in doing so, it gives your own pain a deeper meaning.In many Indian villages, community healers often grandmothers or storytellers would gather people and tell tales at night. They didn't hold degrees. But their words had the power to mend broken spirits. Their stories weren't about heroes in palaces. They were about ordinary people who fell, failed, and still stood up again. These stories were the soul's medicine.

Today, in a world full of noise, we've forgotten to pause and share. We scroll, we type, but we rarely speak from the heart. It's time to return to the campfire to gather, to speak, and to listen. Not to impress, but to connect. Maybe your story could be the spark that lights someone else's way out of the dark. Maybe, just maybe, your voice is the bridge that someone else needs to cross their pain. Speak. Not because you're unbroken, but because someone else needs to know it's possible to survive and thrive just like you did. There's something deeply comforting about someone who simply shows up. Not with answers. Not with grand solutions. But with a steady heart and an open hand. In a world obsessed with perfection, presence is a rare gift. We often think we need to have everything figured out before we can help someone else. We believe we must be fully healed before offering healing. But this isn't true. In fact, it's the very cracks in our lives that let the light through and that light can guide others. In psychological terms, this is called **attuned listening** being mentally, emotionally, and physically present with another person. Studies from the University of Oregon show that when someone feels truly heard, their brain activity shifts. Cortisol (the stress hormone) drops, while oxytocin (the connection hormone) rises. They feel safer, calmer, more hopeful not because their problem was fixed, but because someone cared enough to really be there.

I once heard a story from a small village in Gujarat. A widowed woman in her 60s lost both her sons in a tragic accident. She stopped speaking. Neighbours tried everything like food, doctors, prayers but she remained silent. One day, a young girl from the village sat beside her and just held her hand. She said nothing. She came back the next day. And the next. After two weeks, the woman finally whispered, "Thank you for not leaving me alone." That was the beginning of her healing. We underestimate the power of just being with someone. We think we have to say the right words. But sometimes, your silent company speaks louder than any advice ever could.

You don't need to be a psychologist or a guru. You just need to care. Presence is what we're all really hungry for. In our fast-scrolling, hyper-distracted lives, it's rare to find someone who will pause everything to truly look at you, listen to you, and be with you. But when we find that, we remember what it means to be human. Think about it: haven't your most healing moments often come not from a perfect solution, but from someone saying, "I'm here"?

When you choose to be present - fully, honestly and you become a lighthouse for others. You don't chase away their storms, but you help them navigate it. And often, that's more than enough. You don't have to shine the brightest. Just don't disappear. There is a beautiful truth that often goes unnoticed, when we help someone else, we also help ourselves. It might seem surprising, but modern science and ancient Indian wisdom both agree on this. Giving, caring, and supporting others isn't just good for the world, it's medicine for the soul.

In our Indian tradition, there is a Sanskrit phrase, **"Atithi Devo Bhava"**, which means "The guest is like God." But this idea goes even deeper. In many villages, elders say that when you help a person in need, especially someone broken or hurting, you are helping a part of yourself that once cried in silence. You might not see it at first, but your spirit knows and it starts to heal.

Modern psychology explains this through something called **"helper's high."** It's a real feeling, a wave of joy, peace, and energy that flows through your body when you do something kind. Scientists at Stanford University discovered that when we give, our brain releases dopamine (which makes us feel pleasure) and oxytocin (which helps us feel love and connection). It's like nature's reward system. the more you give, the better you feel. Take for example the story of *Anupama*, a young teacher from Bihar. She lost her only brother to depression. For months, she was drowned in guilt and sadness, thinking, "If only I had done something." But slowly, she began volunteering at a local school where children from poor backgrounds came to study. At first, she could barely smile. But every day, as she helped one child with reading or another with homework, something shifted. The pain didn't go away but it transformed. "I feel like I'm giving meaning to my brother's memory," she said. Today, Anupama has started a small foundation that gives books and emotional support to children in rural areas. Helping others doesn't always mean starting a big movement. Sometimes, it's just standing beside someone when they feel lost. Or cooking a meal for someone who's grieving. Or simply calling a friend to say, "I'm thinking of you." These actions may feel small, but to someone in darkness, they can be life-changing.

The Bhagavad Gita beautifully says, *"When a man responds to the sorrows of others as though they were his own, he has attained the highest state of human consciousness."* This is the kind of light we are meant to spread not by preaching or showing off, but by quietly being present, kind, and real. When you carry the torch of kindness, you light up not only another's path but also your own. You begin to realize: your pain was not just meant to break you. It was meant to soften you, so you could hold someone else's pain with love and in that act, something magical happens your soul smiles. Sometimes we think we are too small to make a big difference. We wonder, "What can one person do in such a large world?" But the truth is even a single spark can light a thousand lamps. One person's kindness can begin a chain reaction that changes not just lives, but entire generations. In Indian families, values often pass down quietly not through lectures, but through daily actions. A grandmother waking up before sunrise to prepare food for the family, even after a sleepless night. A father walking miles to earn just enough to educate his daughter. A sister sacrificing her dreams so her brother can study. These stories are not rare. They are everywhere which is unnoticed, unspoken, but full of light. Let me tell you about *Mohammed Salim*, a man from West Bengal. He was once a rickshaw-puller who barely earned enough to survive. But he used part of his income every month to buy books for poor children in his slum. At first, only two or three kids came. He didn't stop. Ten years later, one of those children *Rekha* became a school teacher. She now teaches 120 kids in the same slum.

This is the ripple effect. Salim did not know his small act would bloom into something so powerful. But it did.

Psychology has a term for this: **"prosocial behavior spread."** Studies show that when one person performs an act of kindness, it often inspires at least three others to do something kind too. This ripple keeps moving outward, like waves in water. A 2010 study from the University of California proved this: kindness is contagious - emotionally, biologically, and socially. Think of your own life. Maybe someone once believed in you when no one else did. Maybe a teacher saw your spark. Or a stranger helped you when you were stranded. These people may not remember what they did, but you do. Their light entered your life and shaped who you are today. Now, imagine becoming that person for someone else. You don't need a microphone or a stage. You don't need money or fame. What you need is presence, compassion, and courage. The courage to show up even when you're tired. To love, even when you've been hurt. To give even when you're healing. Because when you do that, your small acts start traveling silently through hearts, homes, and histories. You might not see the end of your ripple, but rest assured, it's reaching far and wide and in that way, your light becomes eternal. Pain has a strange way of shaping people. It can either break them, or make them. But the most inspiring people are those who took their wounds and turned them into wisdom not just for themselves, but for the world around them.

In ancient India, pain was not seen as something to be hidden or erased. It was honored as a teacher. The **Upanishads** speak of suffering not as punishment, but as a doorway to deeper understanding. The wise rishis believed that only through going within facing your inner darkness could true light be born. That light, once awakened, becomes a torch for others.

Let's take the story of *Sudha Murthy*, one of India's most respected philanthropists and writers. Her life was not always full of praise and success. As a young engineer, she faced gender bias, loneliness, and rejection. But instead of growing bitter, she grew kinder. She built schools, helped women, and wrote books that touched millions of hearts. Her early wounds became the foundation of her wisdom and through that, she became a light for countless others. This pattern repeats in so many lives maybe even yours. A difficult childhood can make someone a better parent. A failed exam can make someone more disciplined. A broken heart can make someone more understanding. The key is not to hide the wound, but to heal it and then share the lesson it taught.

Modern psychology agrees. Dr. Richard Tedeschi, a leading psychologist in trauma recovery, according to his research, many people who suffer deeply end up becoming more resilient, emotionally aware, and committed to meaningful goals. In fact, some of the most generous social workers, teachers, and leaders come from difficult pasts. Their wisdom was not bought, it was earned.

In Indian culture, we are taught that life is not always fair but our response to it can be beautiful. This idea is echoed in the **Bhagavad Gita**, where Krishna tells Arjuna: "Do your duty without attachment to the result." That includes the duty of healing, the duty of sharing your strength, the duty of being there for others, even when life has tested you. So, ask yourself: what have your wounds taught you? Maybe you learned the value of patience because someone close to you battled illness. Maybe you discovered inner strength because you had to survive alone. Maybe you learned to forgive, because carrying anger only hurt you more. Each of these lessons is sacred. Each of them can guide someone else. When we open our stories, not in bitterness, but in courage, we give others a map. We say, "I've been there. You're not alone. And it gets better." You don't need to be a saint to teach. You only need to be honest.

Because honesty is light and light, once shared, never dims. In a quiet village in West Bengal, there lived an elderly woman known simply as "Didima." No one knew her full name, and she never spoke about her past. But what everyone remembered was the food she served every evening. Rain or shine, Didima would light a small fire near the community banyan tree and cook simple rice and lentils. The poor, the lonely, and the forgotten came. She fed them with love, no questions asked. It wasn't until after her death that someone found her old diary. In it, she had written about losing her husband and two sons in a tragic flood decades ago. She had been left with nothing but grief and silence. But one day, after almost giving up on life, she remembered how her mother once told her, "When your heart breaks, let the light leak out through the cracks." So she did. She took her pain and poured it into the fire. Every meal she cooked wasn't just food. It was her offering to the world, a way of saying, "I may have lost everything, but I can still give something." Her story, though small and never famous, became legendary in that village. Children still grow up hearing about her. This is the power of silent service. Didima never needed applause, nor did she ever seek it. She healed quietly, but her kindness spoke louder than any speech. Her flame became a beacon not of charity, but of shared humanity. In psychology, there's a term called "vicarious resilience." It describes the emotional strength we gather by witnessing someone else's courage. Didima gave her village that gift. People who saw her never complained about their lives in the same way again. They realized healing didn't require a hospital. Sometimes, it just needs a heart willing to serve. In a small town in Tamil Nadu, there was a schoolteacher named Mr. Raghavan. He wasn't famous or rich. In fact, he struggled to make ends meet. But he had one thing: a heart full of patience and hope for his students. One of his students was a quiet boy named Arjun. Arjun's family was poor, and he was often bullied at school. He was so shy that he barely spoke in class and often sat alone. Most teachers would have written him off as "slow" or "trouble," but Mr. Raghavan saw something else: a hidden spark. Every day, after the final bell, Mr. Raghavan would spend time with Arjun. He'd patiently explain lessons, listen to his worries, and encourage him to believe in himself. Slowly, Arjun's confidence grew. Years later, Arjun became the first in his family to graduate from college and even started a small business helping other children with their studies. What's beautiful about this story is that Mr. Raghavan never sought praise. To him, teaching was not just a job. It was a chance to bring light into someone's dark world. His belief in Arjun became a lifeline, and it showed how a single person's faith can change the course of a life. From a psychological perspective, this example aligns with a concept called "social support theory." This theory tells us that when people feel cared for and supported, they build resilience against life's challenges. Mr. Raghavan's kindness gave Arjun a safety net, a place to recover and grow.

Research from Indian educational institutions confirms that teachers who build strong emotional bonds with students create environments where children thrive. These bonds can be more powerful than textbooks or exams. They offer a sense of belonging and purpose crucial elements for mental health. Mr. Raghavan's story reminds us that sometimes being the light for others is as simple as showing up, listening, and believing. You don't need grand gestures to create deep impact. Sometimes, your consistent presence is enough. In our fast-paced lives, it's easy to forget that small acts of attention and kindness are powerful. But for someone like Arjun, that daily attention was a lifeline. It's a reminder that we all have the ability to be a beacon for someone else whether it's a student, a sibling, a friend, or a stranger.

So, if you've ever felt powerless in the face of someone else's pain, remember Mr. Raghavan. Your patience and belief can become the gentle light that guides someone from darkness into hope. And when you do this, you become more than a teacher, a friend, or a helper, you become a true light in the world. Think about a time when you opened up to someone about a difficult experience. Maybe it was a personal failure, loss, or fear. How did that feel? Scary? Vulnerable? Maybe, yes. But also, maybe you felt lighter, freer, like a burden had been lifted. That's no accident. Research in psychology shows that telling your story, especially about hardships, can help you process emotions and find meaning. This is called "narrative therapy." When we give our pain words, we start to understand it better, and that understanding can bring healing. But here's the magic when you share your story with others, you create a connection. Others who have faced similar struggles feel seen, heard, and less alone. In India, where many still find it hard to talk openly about mental health or personal pain, sharing stories is even more powerful. It breaks silence and stigma. It becomes a quiet revolution of empathy. Take the example of a young woman from Maharashtra, who after battling depression, started sharing her journey on community radio. Her voice reached thousands of listeners who felt inspired to seek help or just feel less isolated. She became a beacon, not because she was perfect or had all the answers, but because she was brave enough to be real. Stories connect us in a way that facts and advice cannot. When we hear someone's lived experience, it awakens empathy in our hearts. Neuroscience shows that listening to stories activates the parts of our brain responsible for understanding others' emotions and making moral judgments. This empathetic connection is the seed of kindness and support. So, how can you use your story to become a light? You don't need a huge audience or a stage. It can be as simple as talking honestly with a friend, writing a letter, or even journaling your feelings. Every act of sharing chips away at the walls of isolation. Remember, your story isn't just about pain, it's about resilience, learning, and growth. When you share it, you offer a path for others to walk, showing them that darkness can be crossed, that failure can turn into fuel. You might never know how deeply your words will touch someone else's life. But they will. Just like the ancient Indian tradition of passing down wisdom through stories, your experience can be a lamp carried forward, lighting the way for someone else. In a world that often pushes us to "fix" problems quickly or give advice, one of the most overlooked but powerful ways to become the light for others is simply by being present. Not just physically, but emotionally and mentally present. This means listening without interrupting, holding space for someone's pain, and offering your genuine attention without judgment or trying to change their feelings. In Indian families and communities, presence has a deep meaning. Our culture values "saath", togetherness, companionship, and solidarity. When a family member faces grief or hardship, often the greatest comfort comes not from words, but from shared silence, a hand held, or simply sitting beside them through their pain. Studies in social psychology back this up. Researchers find that emotional presence can reduce a person's stress hormones and increase feelings of safety. This is especially vital in times of crisis or emotional turmoil. When you show up fully for someone, you tell their brain, "You are not alone." That message alone can spark hope and healing. Think about the ancient Indian practice of "satsang", gathering in the company of others to listen, share, and find peace. The word itself means "being with truth." In those moments, the power lies not in lectures or advice, but in shared human connection. That connection is what can help someone move from darkness into light. The beauty of presence is that it doesn't require any special skill or training. It requires empathy, patience, and sometimes just humility recognizing that your role is not to fix, but to accompany. Being a light for others doesn't mean you need to have answers or magic fixes. Often, the greatest gift is simply your time and attention. In a society that moves fast, where people often feel isolated despite living in large families or communities, your presence is like a healing balm. This simple truth reminds me of a verse from the Bhagavad Gita, where Krishna says that true support comes through unwavering companionship and presence. It's not the loudest voice or the most dazzling act that shines brightest, but the steady, gentle presence that endures. So, next time someone you care about is struggling, try this: don't rush to give advice. Don't try to solve. Just be there. Listen deeply. Let your presence be the light that helps them find their own way. In this way, the ripple you create is not just for them, but for everyone touched by your kindness, a living chain of light and hope. Every corner of the world has its own stories of people who, despite facing deep struggles, chose to become a light for others. These stories remind us that kindness, resilience, and hope are universal values that cross borders, languages, and cultures.

In Japan, the concept of *kintsugi* beautifully symbolizes this idea. When a precious ceramic breaks, artisans don't throw it away. Instead, they repair it with gold, making the cracks part of its beauty and history. This ancient philosophy teaches that wounds and scars don't diminish value, they enhance it. People who have experienced pain often become uniquely able to support others because their "golden cracks" make them wiser and stronger. In Africa, the tradition of Ubuntu, meaning "I am because we are," highlights the power of community and interconnectedness. People heal and grow not just for themselves but because their wellbeing is tied to others. This African philosophy shows that our light shines brightest when it helps illuminate the whole community. The Native American concept of *walking in balance* reminds us that life's hardships are part of a larger journey toward harmony. Many tribal leaders who endured great personal loss became powerful teachers of peace and resilience, guiding their people with the wisdom gained from their pain.

In Scandinavian countries, the idea of *lagom* meaning "just the right amount" encourages balance in all aspects of life, including emotional wellbeing. People who have struggled often use this principle to guide others toward moderation, mindfulness, and sustainable kindness. These examples from around the world all share a common truth: suffering can be a powerful source of empathy and strength. When people choose to use their pain to help others, they create ripples far beyond their own lives. Psychological research from global studies shows that communities that encourage sharing personal stories and supporting one another recover faster from trauma and hardship. Collective healing is often stronger than going it alone. You don't have to travel far to feel connected to this universal spirit. Every culture teaches, in its own way, that becoming the light for others is a sacred gift, one that anyone can give. The world's great leaders, thinkers, and healers all share one thing: they turned their pain into purpose. Their light crosses oceans, time, and language to remind us that no matter where we come from, we all have the power to brighten someone else's path. So, when you face darkness, remember the many lights shining around the world. You are part of a global story, a story of hope, healing, and the courage to become the light for others. India is a land full of stories about ordinary people who faced immense struggles but chose to rise and become lights for others. These heroes didn't wait for perfect moments or flawless lives. They acted from their pain and made a difference. Their journeys teach us that anyone can become a guiding light, no matter how dark their past.

Take the example of **Dr. B.R. Ambedkar**, who was born into a community oppressed for centuries. Despite facing rejection, poverty, and discrimination, he dedicated his entire life to fighting injustice and building a fair society. Ambedkar's personal hardships didn't break him, they fueled his determination. His work gave voice to millions and transformed India's social fabric. Today, his light guides those striving for equality and dignity.

Then there's **Kiran Bedi**, India's first woman police officer. She grew up in a society that didn't easily accept women in such roles. But instead of giving up, she broke every glass ceiling with courage and empathy. Kiran Bedi's story is about turning societal barriers into opportunities to serve and protect others. Her light inspires countless women to chase their dreams and help communities heal.

We also remember **Mother Teresa**, whose life was a profound example of becoming light through selfless service. Coming from a small village in Albania, she moved to India and chose to live among the poorest of the poor in Kolkata's slums. Mother Teresa's compassion was her strength. Even though she faced criticism and immense challenges, she never stopped. Her light still shines in the hearts of those who believe in kindness and unconditional love. You don't have to be famous to become a light. Every day, countless Indians quietly embody this spirit. A mother who sacrifices to educate her children, a teacher who goes beyond textbooks to inspire hope, a young person volunteering in their village, all become ripples of light in their own communities. Becoming the light for others means turning your wounds into wisdom and your fears into courage. It means choosing to shine even when the path is hard. In India, leadership has often been seen not just as power or authority, but as a sacred responsibility. The ancient *Raj Dharma* (duty of a king) was about protecting and serving the people, not ruling over them. This idea—that true leaders are those who serve others—holds a timeless lesson for all of us. When you choose to become a light for others, you begin to awaken your own inner leader. Leadership through service starts with empathy - really feeling what others feel. This is not about grand speeches or titles; it's about listening deeply, understanding silently, and acting gently. This is alive even today, in families, schools, and communities where elders guide the young not by command but by example and care. Life often tests us with challenges that feel heavy and overwhelming. In those moments, it's natural to feel alone or defeated. But what if those very struggles could become the source of your greatest strength the fuel that lights the way for others? This is the essence of becoming a leader through service, especially when you transform your pain into a beacon for someone else's hope. Imagine your struggles as seeds planted deep in the soil. With care and attention, they sprout into beautiful trees whose shade and fruit nourish others. When you openly share your story - the setbacks, the doubts, and the eventual growth you create a connection that is both powerful and healing. It shows others they are not alone, and that difficulties can be overcome. On a personal level, when you use your experience to guide others, you begin to see your own life with new meaning. You stop seeing yourself as broken or weak and start recognizing the value in your journey. This shift in perspective is powerful because it creates hope - the kind that is rooted not in fantasy, but in lived experience. Think about the simple acts that can make a big difference: speaking honestly about your setbacks during a team meeting, mentoring a young person who is facing similar challenges, or simply listening without judgment when someone shares their pain. These moments ripple out, creating a culture of empathy and courage. Your personal challenge doesn't just belong to you. It becomes part of a larger story that can uplift many. The light you create by facing your darkness shines further than you can imagine. This journey is not always easy. There will be times when you feel exhausted or unsure. But remember, even the tallest trees grow slowly, one ring at a time. Leadership through transformation is a steady process filled with small victories and moments of grace. As you keep moving forward, hold onto the belief that your pain can be a gift. When you lead with your whole heart, others will find strength in your example and learn to face their own challenges with courage.

By turning your struggles into a source of light, you are not just changing your life. You are helping to build a kinder, stronger world. Sometimes, when we think of leadership or making a difference, we imagine grand gestures or big projects. But the truth is, many of the most powerful changes in communities start with small, simple acts. This is the beauty of leadership through kindness - it doesn't require titles, money, or fame. It only asks for your willingness to step forward, however small the step may be. A simple example comes from rural India, where many women have started self-help groups to support each other in times of crisis. These groups often begin with one person offering encouragement or practical help to another. Slowly, they grow into strong networks that empower members financially, emotionally, and socially. This grassroots leadership has lifted countless families out of poverty and despair.

Globally, too, small acts of kindness have changed lives. During natural disasters, for example, ordinary people stepping up to help strangers has repeatedly made a huge difference. After the 2015 Nepal earthquake, volunteers organized food and medical supplies, helped rebuild homes, and provided emotional support to survivors. Their leadership, born from compassion rather than position, saved lives and rebuilt hope. These stories teach us that leadership isn't about being perfect or having all the answers.

It's about showing up, caring, and doing what you can with what you have. When you do this, you inspire others to believe that they too can make a difference. This creates a culture where kindness and courage grow naturally. On a personal note, I remember a time when a small act of kindness from a stranger deeply touched me. I was struggling with self-doubt and fear, unsure if I could continue my journey.

A simple smile and encouraging words from a fellow traveler gave me the strength to keep going. That moment stayed with me, reminding me how powerful kindness can be. So, as you continue your journey of becoming a light for others, remember: every smile, every word of encouragement, every moment of listening deeply, can spark a wave of change. These small acts build bridges, heal wounds, and inspire hope.

8. The Art of Not Giving Up

There's a day we all remember, even if we never speak of it. A day that lives quietly in the corners of our minds. Not because it was loud or dramatic, but because it was still heavy. It may have looked ordinary from the outside. A walk to work. A cup of tea left unfinished. A long stare at the ceiling. But inside, something shifted. That was the day your heart whispered, *"What's the point?"* And for a fleeting moment, you believed it.

Maybe you were stuck in a job that hollowed out your spirit. Maybe you were chasing a dream that seemed foolish in everyone else's eyes. Or maybe, you were just tired — not the kind of tired that sleep cures, but the kind that settles deep in your bones. The tiredness that comes from carrying burdens too big for one person, from pretending too long that everything is fine.

If you've ever been there and many of us have — I want to say something that we don't hear often enough. You are **not** weak for wanting to give up. You are **strong** for still being here. You are strong for trying again today, even if no one sees how hard it is.

Our world glorifies the spotlight. The meteoric rise. The flawless victory. We hear endless stories of people who "made it" overnight, who conquered mountains, who turned their pain into power with one grand gesture. But here's the truth they don't tell you: the real heroes walk in silence. They cry behind closed doors and still go to work. They fall down and stand up, not once, but over and over again. Without applause. Without reward. Just sheer courage.

There's an art to not giving up. It's not painted in bold strokes. It doesn't scream from rooftops. It's quiet. Tender. Deeply personal. It's the decision to take one more breath, to step forward even if your legs are shaking. It's brushing your hair when your soul feels like it's unraveling. It's replying to an email after twenty rejections. It's smiling at a stranger while carrying invisible grief.

These moments, the small ones — they matter. They matter more than the world admits. Because strength doesn't live in the dramatic. It hides in the ordinary. In the morning you opened your eyes when your heart was heavy. In the hour you kept going, even when no one clapped.

You don't have to scale the entire mountain today. You don't need to rebuild your life in a week. You just need to take one honest, human step. And then another. And another. That's how comebacks are made. Not by magic. But by motion. Not in noise. But in stillness. You're not alone in your struggle, even if your pain feels invisible. The truth is, most people are fighting silent battles you'll never see. Modern psychology has a term for what you might be feeling — **"learned helplessness."** It was first identified by Dr. Martin Seligman in the 1960s. He found that when people (or animals) are subjected to repeated failure or hardship with no control over the outcome, they begin to believe that nothing they do matters. Eventually, they stop trying — even when the possibility of escape or success becomes real.

Sound familiar?

That numbness. That quiet surrender. That voice inside that says, *"Why bother?"* — it's not laziness. It's not weakness. It's the brain's tragic way of protecting you from further disappointment. Your mind is saying, *"I don't want you to be hurt again."* But in doing so, it shuts down your will to try. Long before you knew your name, you inherited something far more powerful than your surname, a silent script of emotions, beliefs, and fears passed down through generations. You didn't choose it. But it chose you.

Maybe your mother never said she was afraid. But you saw it in the way she hesitated before speaking up. Maybe your father never cried. But you felt the weight of his unspoken grief in the room. Maybe your grandfather lived through poverty, and even though you were born in a different world, you still feel guilty every time you spend money on yourself.

These aren't just family patterns, they are emotional legacies. Psychologists call it **intergenerational transmission of trauma**. It means that we often carry the wounds of those who came before us, even without fully understanding them. Our body keeps the score, a phrase coined by trauma expert Dr. Bessel van der Kolk and it remembers pain, even when our conscious mind forgets and so we move through life with invisible burdens like fear of being abandoned, constant pressure to prove our worth, shame around joy, or an inability to express love freely. And we wonder why happiness feels foreign, why we sabotage our progress, or why relationships confuse us.

To truly *become you*, you must recognize what parts of your emotional blueprint were **borrowed**, not **built**. This doesn't mean blaming your parents or resenting your past. It means becoming an emotional detective in your own story. It means asking yourself: *Is this feeling mine? Or did I inherit it?* You might be shocked by how much of your emotional life is an echo of someone else's pain.

But here's the most beautiful part, emotional inheritance is not destiny. Awareness is your first act of rebellion. Healing is your first act of freedom. The moment you pause and ask why, you begin to break the chain. Your ancestors survived wars, famines, heartbreaks, colonization, exile, and betrayals. You are their dream come alive. But you are also the bridge. You are the first in your line who gets to stop surviving and start living.

When you heal, you do not heal alone. You heal forward. You heal backward. You become the ancestor your future generations will thank not because you were perfect, but because you were **conscious**. From the moment we become aware, life begins to tell us stories. Stories about who we are, what we deserve, what is possible. These stories live in our mind like scripts in a play, some written by our parents, some by teachers, some by friends, and some by strangers long forgotten.

"You're not good enough."

"You'll never succeed."
"You always mess things up."
"Love is dangerous."
"Being different means being alone."

Do these sound familiar? Maybe not in these exact words, but the feeling behind them is the invisible weight does. These stories don't just whisper in the background; they shape your emotions, your decisions, your relationships. They build the walls you live behind.

But here's the thing about stories: **They are not facts. They are narratives and narratives can be changed.**

Think about it. If you hear a story often enough, you start to believe it is truth. But stories are simply interpretations, a way of making sense of the chaos of life. And like any story, they can be edited, challenged, rewritten. What if the story you've been telling yourself isn't the whole story? What if there is a hidden chapter where you are brave, loved, enough exactly as you are? Rewriting your inner story isn't about pretending. It's about **seeing clearly** — seeing both the old, limiting chapters and the new, hopeful possibilities. It is about becoming the author of your own life, not just a character trapped in someone else's script. This process starts with listening deeply and honestly to the stories you carry. Then, with courage, you ask:

"Is this story serving me or limiting me?"

"Where did this story come from?"

"What story do I want to live instead?"

Every small moment of choosing a new story builds a new identity. Like planting seeds in fertile soil, your mind slowly grows a new landscape of belief and possibility and when your story changes, your world changes. You begin to live not as a victim of your past but as a creator of your future. You begin to recognize your strengths, your worth, and your infinite potential. This is how you become you — one story, one choice, one truth at a time. In a world that never stops talking, scrolling, connecting, and competing, solitude often feels like a punishment. We fear it, avoid it, and fill every quiet moment with noise — a phone, a distraction, a rush.

But solitude is not loneliness. It is a profound gift, a secret door to your true self. When you step away from the noise of the world, you meet yourself in ways impossible in a crowd. Solitude is where you face your fears without disguise. It is where your heart whispers its deepest truths, and your mind begins to untangle the knots of confusion. In solitude, the layers you wear to please others or to hide your pain begin to fall away. There is no mask, no performance — only you, raw and real. This rawness can feel uncomfortable, even frightening. Yet, it is in this discomfort that growth happens. Like a seed cracking open beneath the soil, you too must break through your protective shell to reach the light.

Artists, writers, spiritual teachers, and great thinkers throughout history have praised solitude as their greatest ally. It is in silence that creativity flows, clarity emerges, and resilience strengthens. But solitude is not about isolation; it is about **presence** — presence with yourself.

To accept solitude is to learn the art of being with your own thoughts, feelings, and dreams without judgment. It is to listen deeply to your inner voice, that quiet guide that knows your path even when the world seems lost. When you make space for solitude, you cultivate a sanctuary inside — a place you can always return to, no matter what chaos rages outside and from this sanctuary, you begin to live more intentionally. You choose actions that honor your authentic self, not just the expectations of others. Solitude is not emptiness; it is fullness. It is where your soul breathes and your true light shines.

So, if you have been running from solitude, stop. Step

gently into its embrace. Give yourself permission to be alone, and watch how you become whole. We often look for grand moments — the big decisions, the dramatic breakthroughs to define who we are. We wait for a lightning strike of change that will suddenly transform everything.

But real transformation rarely happens in giant leaps. Instead, it is the quiet, almost invisible rhythm of small choices that shapes the core of who you become. Every day, you face countless tiny decisions: what to focus on, how to speak to yourself, whether to keep trying or give up. These choices may seem insignificant alone, but they add up like drops of water carving stone over years.

The challenge is that small choices don't feel powerful in the moment. When you skip one workout, eat one unhealthy meal, or lose your temper once, it feels like no big deal. But these moments accumulate silently, pushing your life in one direction or another. The good news is that the reverse is true too. By consciously choosing small actions aligned with your true self, you build momentum. These tiny victories become habits, habits become character, and character becomes destiny.

This is why patience and persistence are secret

superpowers. Change takes time — often years of steady, quiet work but it is reliable and lasting.

The people you admire the ones who inspire you with their courage, wisdom, or kindness are those who have mastered the art of small consistent choices. They show up day after day, making the hard but right choice, even when no one else is watching.

You have that power too.

Start where you are. Pick one small choice today that honors your deepest values. Maybe it's pausing before you react, choosing gratitude over complaint, or dedicating five minutes to a dream you've been neglecting. The magic is in consistency, not perfection. or decades, we believed our DNA was our destiny that the genes we inherit rigidly defined who we are. But modern science has rewritten this story in profound ways.

Now we will talk about **epigenetics**, the study of how environmental factors, behaviors, and experiences can switch genes on or off, influencing how they express themselves without changing the underlying DNA sequence. Imagine your genes as a vast library, with epigenetics acting like bookmarks and highlighters that tell your body which pages to read and which to skip. This means your lifestyle, diet, stress levels, and even thoughts can affect the activity of your genes, shaping your physical and mental health, and potentially even passing some effects to future generations. Groundbreaking studies show that chronic stress can leave chemical marks on genes regulating the body's stress response, making individuals more vulnerable to anxiety and depression. Conversely, positive experiences like nurturing relationships or mindfulness can foster beneficial epigenetic changes, promoting resilience and well-being. One famous example is the research on children of Holocaust survivors, who displayed epigenetic changes linked to trauma suggesting that life experiences can echo through generations.

This insight shatters the fatalistic view of "I was born this way" and opens a powerful truth:

You hold a measure of control over your biology through your choices and environment.

Epigenetics tells us that personal transformation is not just psychological or behavioral but also biological — a dance between your genes and the world you live in.

This fusion of biology and environment means:

- You are never locked into inherited patterns.

- Every day offers a chance to write new stories in your body's script.

- Self-care is a profound act of gene expression management.

- So, when you work to become a better version of yourself, remember it's not just about willpower or habits.

You're reshaping the expression of your very genes, turning potential into reality.

Your transformation is not only mental or emotional. It's molecular, biological, even generational and that knowledge brings a deep, humbling respect for your power and responsibility. You are the curator of your genetic legacy. Epigenetics is the scientific key to unlocking the eternal possibility of becoming. Did you know your stomach has a brain of its own? It's called the **gut-brain connection**. Your gut isn't just for digesting food. It actually sends messages to your brain all day long! Inside your gut lives trillions of tiny helpers called **microbes** or **good bacteria**. These little creatures break down your food, fight bad germs, and even help control your mood. Scientists have found that a healthy gut can make you feel happier and less anxious. That's because these bacteria produce chemicals like **serotonin**, which is often called the "feel-good" hormone. But if your gut is unhappy maybe because of too much junk food, stress, or antibiotics. It sends confusing signals to your brain. This can lead to problems like feeling sad, stressed, or foggy in your mind.

Taking care of your gut is like watering a plant. You need to feed it the right foods: fiber from fruits and vegetables, yogurt with live cultures, and fermented foods like pickles or kimchi. Drinking enough water and avoiding too much sugar or processed foods helps too. Even simple habits like chewing slowly and enjoying your meals can help your gut do its best work. The gut-brain connection teaches us that **your mind and body are deeply linked**. When you care for your gut, you care for your mood and brain health too.

This means your happiness is not just in your head. It starts from your belly! By paying attention to what you eat and how you treat your gut, you are strengthening a powerful bridge between your body and mind. Your gut is your second brain, cheering you on quietly — if you listen carefully. Have you ever noticed how a certain song can instantly change your mood? Or how being in complete silence can feel both peaceful and a little strange? Sound is one of the most powerful forces around us, yet we often take it for granted. It can heal, motivate, or even harm us.

But sound is more than just music. Everyday noises like traffic, chatter, or construction can stress your brain if they're too loud or constant. This is called **noise pollution**, and it affects your ability to focus, sleep well, and even your heart health. On the other hand, **silence** gives your brain a chance to rest and reset. In silence, your mind can wander, solve problems, or just breathe.

Some studies show that spending even a few minutes in silence can reduce stress hormones and lower your blood pressure. This is why meditation often uses silence or very soft sounds to help calm the mind. Your brain is wired to respond to sound. It can uplift or drain your energy. By choosing what sounds you surround yourself with, you take control of your mental state.

Try to listen to soothing music when you need calm, or energetic beats when you need motivation. Also, make space for silence. Turn off your phone, find a quiet spot, and just breathe. Sound and silence together create a balance that keeps your mind strong and peaceful.

Next time you feel overwhelmed, ask yourself what sounds are filling your world? Are they helping or hurting you? Learning to use sound wisely is a secret tool to improve your happiness and focus every day. Smiling is something we do every day. Sometimes when we're happy, sometimes just to be polite. But did you know smiling is actually a powerful tool for your mind and body? When you smile, your brain releases **endorphins** and **serotonin**, natural chemicals that make you feel good and reduce stress. This means that even if you're feeling down, forcing a smile can trick your brain into feeling happier.

Scientists call this the **facial feedback hypothesis**, the idea that your facial expressions can influence your emotions. Smiling also lowers your heart rate and helps your body relax. It's like a mini workout for your mood! Beyond your own feelings, smiling is contagious. When you smile at someone, their brain often responds by smiling back. This simple exchange can create a positive chain reaction, lifting the mood of both people. Smiling improves your social connections, making you appear more approachable and friendly. This can open doors in friendships, work, and even romantic relationships. Interestingly, studies show that people who smile more often tend to live longer and have better health. That's because smiling strengthens your immune system and lowers blood pressure. Even in difficult times, smiling can provide strength and hope. So next time you feel stressed or worried, try smiling even if you don't feel like it. You might be surprised how much it can shift your day, your mindset, and even your life.

Smiling is free, simple, and powerful, a small habit with big rewards. Life will test you in ways you never expect. It will push you beyond what you think are your limits, knock you down when you least expect it, and sometimes whisper in your ear that maybe it's time to quit. Those moments are the hardest. When your heart feels heavy, and the road ahead seems too dark to travel. But here's the truth: the real secret to success and happiness isn't about never falling. It's about choosing to stand up, again and again, even when every part of you wants to give in.

Not giving up doesn't mean you have to be perfect or never make mistakes. It doesn't mean you won't feel tired or scared. It simply means that no matter how unclear or difficult your path becomes, you keep moving forward. You learn from the falls, you grow stronger from the pain, and you believe that every small step, no matter how tiny — brings you closer to where you want to be. It's in those small steps, repeated over and over, that real change happens.

Imagine a small seed buried deep in the soil. It's dark, heavy, and the soil above feels like a wall too high to climb. But inside that tiny seed, there is a quiet power — the will to grow. It pushes a small root down to find water, and then a fragile shoot upward, searching for sunlight. The seed doesn't give up because it can't see the sky yet. It keeps growing, day by day, breaking through the dirt, bending but never breaking. One day, it becomes a tall tree that stands strong and tall, providing shade and shelter to many. Like that seed, your strength lies in growing quietly and steadily, even when you can't see the end.

So, when you feel overwhelmed or ready to give up, remember this: every champion you admire was once a beginner who faced fear, failure, and doubt. Every story of success is built on countless moments where someone chose courage over comfort, persistence over surrender. Those moments, though often unseen, are where greatness begins.

The art of not giving up is, above all, the art of believing in yourself — even when others don't believe in you, even when the world feels against you. That quiet belief, that small flame inside your heart, is your greatest power. It is what will carry you through storms, what will help you rise after every fall.

Keep going. Keep believing. Your story is not over. In fact, it is just beginning. The best chapters, the most beautiful pages, are waiting for you to write them. And with every step you take, you become the hero of your own life — unstoppable, unbreakable, and unstoppable.

9. The Light You Carry Forward

In the quiet hours before dawn, when the world still holds its breath, there exists a tiny spark inside each of us. It is not a flash of brilliance or a burst of confidence, but a gentle glow like soft, steady, and knowing. This glow is the light you carry forward. It may not always be visible to those around you, yet it guides every step you take, even when the path is shrouded in mist. It is born from your experiences, shaped by every triumph and every setback, and it whispers to you that your story has not ended.In the same way, your inner light does not have to blaze like a wildfire. A quiet pulse is enough to keep you moving, especially when doubt and fear loom large. The moments when you muster the courage to rise from bed despite a faltering heart amount to more than mere survival, they are the refrains of your inner lighthouse at work.

This light does not demand applause or recognition. It grows stronger in secluded moments: the early morning ritual of brewing tea, the minutes spent breathing in and out, the silent resolve to show kindness even when you feel empty. Each time you choose compassion over criticism, you feed your spark. Each time you choose hope over despair, you nurture its warmth. And each time you choose presence over distraction, you allow your light to shine more clearly.

Imagine walking through a forest at dusk, uncertain which way leads out. Then you spot a single firefly dancing ahead. It is no grand spectacle, but it lights the ground at your feet and hints at the path forward. That tiny creature carries its own light, just as you carry yours. You may not see its entire glow, but you sense its invitation: keep going, one step at a time. The firefly does not flicker because it is unimportant; it flickers because that is how it survives. In your own life, your light may flicker in exhaustion or grief, yet it never quite goes out.

This light carries stories. It contains the memory of moments when you laughed despite tears, when you forgave instead of holding grudges, when you reached out to someone else while longing for help yourself. These stories become part of your beam, enriching its texture and depth. And just as a lighthouse's light has traveled through countless nights, your own light has passed through trials, reshaped by each experience and made more resilient. You may wonder how to keep this light alive when life's winds howl. The answer lies in small acts, gentle stoking of your inner fire. Remind yourself daily of something that makes you feel alive: the softness of a pillow beneath your head, the sound of birdsong at sunrise, or the taste of mango juice on a warm afternoon. When you pause to acknowledge those moments, you become the keeper of your light. You tend to it without needing anything dramatic to happen. The truth is, no one is born knowing how to heal. We learn it slowly, painfully, through trial and error. And often, the first thing we have to unlearn is the idea that we are beyond redemption. That we are too broken, too late, too far gone to ever feel whole again. These lies don't come from truth—they come from fear. And fear has a loud voice. It tells us that because we've failed, we *are* a failure. Because we've been hurt, we *deserve* that hurt. But healing begins the moment we start questioning that voice. When we ask ourselves, "What if I'm not too broken? What if this is just a chapter, not the whole book?"

Forgiveness, especially self-forgiveness, is not an act of forgetting. It's not about erasing the past. It's about choosing not to let that past control the future. It's saying, "I did the best I could with what I knew then. And now I know better, so I'll do better." That's not weakness. That's evolution. You're allowed to outgrow who you were. You're allowed to change your mind, to shift your direction, to walk away from stories that no longer serve you. This is not hypocrisy, it's humanity. Even the moon changes shape every night, and yet it never stops shining.

So often, we wait for permission to be at peace. We think we need someone else to tell us we're worthy. That we're forgiven. That we're allowed to move on. But no one else gets to decide that. The most powerful permission slip is the one you write for yourself. "I forgive myself." "I'm allowed to begin again." "I am not only what happened to me, I am what I choose next."

Think of a river. No matter how many stones or obstacles lie in its path, it doesn't stop. It flows over, around, sometimes even through. It carves canyons. It reshapes landscapes. And sometimes, it changes course entirely. But it always keeps moving. Your spirit is like that river. You might not be able to undo what's already been done, but you can decide what shape your future will take. You can become something new.

Science supports this too. Studies on self-compassion have found that people who practice forgiveness not just for others, but for themselves tend to have lower anxiety, better relationships, and improved physical health. The act of forgiving activates the parasympathetic nervous system, the part of us that calms, restores, and heals. In other words, forgiveness isn't just a nice idea, it's a medicine for the soul and the body.

But like any medicine, it takes time. Some days you'll feel like you've forgiven yourself, only to wake up the next morning with regret creeping back in. That's okay. Healing is not a straight line. It's a winding road, with setbacks and breakthroughs tangled together. What matters most is that you stay on the road. That you don't let the guilt win. Because guilt doesn't make you grow, grace does.

So today, even if just for a moment, try this: put your hand on your heart and whisper, "I am still worthy." Not because you've never fallen, but because you've risen. Not because you're perfect, but because you're trying. That trying, that quiet, relentless effort to be better, to love deeper, to live more fully that is the light you carry forward. Trauma doesn't always scream; sometimes it whispers, "Don't trust," "Don't speak," "Don't hope." And yet, every day you wake up and choose to live that is courage. Every time you reach out despite the fear, every time you soften instead of harden, every time you choose love over bitterness, you are healing in the most profound way.We tend to romanticize transformation as something loud and dramatic, like a phoenix rising from flames. But in real life, healing is often quiet. It looks like breathing through a panic attack without calling yourself weak. It looks like reaching out to a friend when everything inside you says isolate. It looks like showing up to work, to family, to yourself. When the past has made you want to disappear. Quiet courage is when no one sees how hard it is, but you do it anyway. It's not about the applause. It's about the integrity of the soul.

Let's talk about something rarely said out loud: you can grieve and grow at the same time. You can miss what hurt you. You can love someone who didn't love you right. You can wish things had turned out differently while still building a new life with both hands. Life is rarely clean. It's messy, overlapping, contradictory. And yet, within that mess, you find meaning. You find you. One of the most liberating truths you will ever realize is this: your pain doesn't make you less worthy of love. In fact, it's often the thing that allows you to *feel* love more deeply. Think about it, why do people who have been broken offer the warmest smiles? Why do those who've known silence listen so well? Why do those who've faced darkness become lanterns for others? Because pain, when faced and felt and not suppressed, transforms you. It doesn't destroy, it refines.

In Indian philosophy, there's a concept called *antaryami*, the inner knower, the guide within. Even when the world outside seems chaotic, that inner knowing remains. It's the quiet voice that tells you to try again. That reassures you that you are more than your mistakes. That whispers, "Keep going," when your strength is gone. Listening to that voice amidst the noise of doubt and fear is a sacred act of self-trust. That trust, that listening, becomes your anchor in the storm.

The world may never fully understand the battles you've fought just to stand where you are today. But that's okay. Your healing is not for the world's validation, it's for your own liberation. Every moment you choose to rise, even shakily, you make a quiet declaration: I am still here. I am still becoming. Letting go is not forgetting. It is not pretending that the pain didn't exist or the betrayal didn't cut deep. Letting go is not weakness, and it is not about excusing the harm done. It's not about saying, "It didn't matter." It mattered. But what matters more now is your peace, your energy, your life. Holding on to what broke you only gives the past a permanent seat in your present. Letting go, in truth, is a brave and sacred rebellion against the weight that no longer serves you. In Indian mythology, the river Ganga is considered sacred not only because of her divinity but because she keeps moving. She carries prayers and pain, ashes and flowers, but she does not hold on to them. She flows. She flows not because it is easy, but because stagnation would mean death. So must we learn the art of letting go - not to forget, but to flow. To carry the lessons, not the poison. You may ask, "But how do I let go when the memory still haunts me?" Here's a truth most people won't tell you: healing is not an event; it's a practice. You let go not once, but again and again. Every time your mind pulls you back to that moment, that person, that regret - you gently say, "Not today." You return to the present. You breathe. You do the next kind thing for yourself. You show up. And that is the slow, quiet miracle of freedom.Often we think that letting go means losing something important. But what if it actually means *returning* to yourself? You see, when you've been entangled in hurt be it from someone else or your own choicesyou start living outside of your soul. You begin performing safety, pretending strength, managing impressions. Letting go means coming back home. To your body. To your truth. To your dreams that you shelved for someone else's comfort. It means whispering to yourself: "I still matter." There is a Sanskrit word- *vairagya* which means detachment, but not in a cold or indifferent way. It means holding life loosely, without grasping or clinging. It means loving without possession, giving without expectation, and grieving without drowning. When you cultivate *vairagya*, you make space for what is meant for you. You stop chasing and start attracting, not from a place of lack, but from a place of wholeness. You no longer beg for love, you embody it.

Letting go also means releasing the version of yourself that you became just to survive. That overly agreeable self, that silent self, that always-pleasing, never-resting self. That version served its purpose, it kept you safe in unsafe places. But now, it is time to thank them... and set them free. You are allowed to evolve. You are allowed to rise. You are allowed to live from your healed, not your wounded, self and yes, sometimes it will hurt. It will feel like tearing your heart from a familiar cage. You'll cry. You'll doubt. But on the other side of that release is a kind of lightness you forgot was possible. The kind of joy that isn't built on conditions. The kind of love that doesn't hurt to hold. The kind of life where you are no longer just surviving, you are beginning to thrive. Pain is not the enemy. Pain is the messenger. It comes wrapped in discomfort and tears, but beneath that is often the one thing we keep avoiding the truth. Pain points us to where healing is needed, where boundaries were crossed, where voices were silenced. It tells us, not that we are broken, but that something in our life needs attention, needs love, needs change. It's life's way of shaking us awake when we've been asleep to our own suffering. In our culture, especially in Indian households, we are often taught to hide pain. "Don't cry in front of others," they say. "Be strong," they insist, as if strength means suppression. But real strength is not in hiding your wounds. It's in daring to feel them fully and still choosing to stand up again. Crying does not make you weak, it makes you human. Vulnerability is not your enemy, it is your passage to transformation.

Take, for example, the lotus. It blooms in muddy water, not in clean ponds. It does not wait for perfect surroundings. It grows despite the mess. Likewise, your pain be it heartbreak, failure, grief, or guilt can become the soil in which your strength is born. Every scar you carry is a reminder that you survived, and every tear that fell was proof that you still care deeply, that your heart still beats with meaning but here is the shift: don't let your pain tur n into your identity. You are not what happened to you. You are what you choose to become after it. That's the difference between staying in the darkness and using it to fuel your light. Pain can imprison you, yes but only if you let it. It can also be the fire that forges a more compassionate, courageous you. It all depends on how you hold it. One of the greatest lessons pain teaches is empathy. The person who has walked through fire often becomes the one who understands others' burn marks without needing explanations. They become the friend who listens without judgment, the stranger who shows unexpected kindness, the mentor who lifts others because they once fell too. Pain, when embraced and alchemized, gives us the power to not just rise alone but to help others rise too and there's another gift: clarity. When you've suffered deeply, the superficial starts to fade. You no longer have time for games, for hollow connections, for living someone else's idea of success. Pain strips away the unnecessary. It brings you back to your core values—love, peace, purpose, authenticity. It asks you, "What really matters to you?" And when you begin to answer, you begin to truly live.

You don't have to glorify pain. You don't have to invite it. But when it arrives as it inevitably will you can welcome it not as a curse but as a teacher. Let it sharpen you, not shatter you. Let it deepen your roots, not drown your spirit. Let it be the force that pushes you beyond the life you settled for into the one you were always meant to live. Most people don't break down because they are weak. They break down because they've been strong for too long, pretending nothing hurts, acting like everything is under control while silently screaming inside. They run not physically, but emotionally. From the past. From the truth. From themselves. They distract themselves with work, with people, with scrolling endlessly through their phones. But no matter how far you run, you carry your pain with you. Healing doesn't begin when the pain ends. It begins when you stop running and turn around to face it.

Imagine sitting silently in a dark room. At first, it's terrifying. All your fears seem louder, your regrets sharper. But if you stay, if you breathe, something shifts. Your eyes adjust. You start seeing in the dark. The shadows become familiar and within that silence, your inner voice begins to speak not the voice of judgment, but the voice of truth. This is the beginning of healing: not when the world changes, but when you're no longer afraid to be alone with yourself. In Indian philosophy, there's a concept called *Swarajya* - self-rule. Before you can rule anything outside, you must rule yourself. That means understanding your triggers, making peace with your wounds, choosing your responses consciously. Most of us are slaves to our past. We react, we lash out, we shut down not because we are bad, but because we are hurting. True freedom isn't escaping your story. It's owning it so powerfully that it no longer controls you.

Healing is not always poetic. It's messy. Some days you'll wake up feeling strong, other days you'll want to crawl back into bed. There will be moments when you feel like you've moved on, and then something a smell, a song, a word will pull you back into the past. That's okay. Healing is not a straight line. It's a spiral. You come back to the same pain, but each time you return, you do so with more awareness, more strength, more understanding. Don't expect others to always understand your healing process. Some people will say, "It's been years, why can't you move on?" But they don't know the weight you carry. They don't see the battles you fight within. Healing isn't a deadline to meet. It's a journey to be honored. Move at your pace. Celebrate every small step. Some days, just getting out of bed is a victory. Some days, being kind to yourself is enough and remember, you don't have to do it alone. Share your story. Find your tribe, the ones who don't try to fix you, but simply sit with you, in silence or in tears. The ones who see your brokenness not as weakness, but as beauty. Healing happens in safe spaces. And sometimes, when you speak your truth, you give someone else permission to heal too. You stop running when you realize that what you feared wasn't the pain. It was the emptiness of not feeling at all. And in that stillness, you find something unexpected: peace. Not the kind that comes from everything being perfect, but the kind that comes from finally accepting yourself, scars and all. That is when the true healing begins. We spend so much of our lives trying to be impressive trying to be liked, accepted, applauded. We wear masks, play roles, say what people want to hear. But beneath it all, what we're really longing for isn't admiration. It's understanding. It's not about someone saying, "You're amazing." It's about someone looking into your eyes and saying, "I see you. I really see you." That moment - rare, raw, and real is where the heart begins to heal.

Many of us grew up in spaces where we were told to "toughen up," to not cry, to not be "too sensitive." So we learned to hide our emotions. We laughed when we wanted to scream. We stayed silent when we wanted to speak. And in doing so, we built walls so high that even we couldn't recognize ourselves behind them. But walls don't just keep pain out. They keep love out too. There's a quiet revolution that begins the day you let someone in not the edited version of you, but the real one. The version with flaws, fears, and past mistakes. When you share your truth, even trembling, even in pieces, and someone doesn't flinch or walk away but stays that moment changes you. You no longer feel alone in your story. You realize that your pain doesn't make you unlovable; it makes you human.

There's power in being truly seen. In Indian literature, there's a term called *Darshan* - the act of seeing and being seen, not just with the eyes but with the soul. When someone offers you *Darshan*, they are not evaluating you. They are witnessing you. And in being witnessed with compassion, parts of you that were buried in shame begin to rise. The child in you, long ignored and dismissed, begins to feel safe again. But the truth is not everyone will be able to see you. Some people will still only see your mistakes, your failures, your worst moments. That's not a reflection of your worth. It's a reflection of their vision. Don't waste your life trying to prove your value to the blind. Seek those whose hearts are open, whose eyes look beyond appearances, who hold space without judgment. These are your people. Protect them. Cherish them. To be understood is one of the most profound experiences a person can have. It tells you that your thoughts matter, your feelings matter, you matter. And sometimes, the first step to being understood by others is understanding yourself. Sit with your own emotions. Ask yourself not just "What am I feeling?" but "Why?" Treat yourself with the same compassion you long for from the world. When you do, you become a mirror for others to do the same. The journey of healing is not just about becoming whole. It's about becoming known to yourself, and to the people who truly care. It's in these honest, vulnerable moments that we find real connection. And connection is the medicine we've always needed. There's a quiet, dangerous myth that floats around us which one that whispers, "You need to fix yourself before you can be loved." It makes us believe that only when we're finally healed, successful, happy, and sorted, we'll be worthy of connection. But the truth is, healing doesn't happen in isolation. It happens in connection and you don't have to be perfect to be loved, you just have to be real.

Think about it: have you ever felt comforted by someone who seemed flawless? Probably not. What truly comforts us is someone who says, "I've been there too." It's not the shiny surface that heals us. It's the raw honesty. When someone opens up about their scars and sits with yours without trying to fix them, a magical thing happens, you feel less broken. You feel human. You feel held. There's immense beauty in shared vulnerability. In Indian culture, there's an old custom of sitting together in silence during sorrow. No words, no advice just presence. Because sometimes, healing isn't in talking; it's in knowing someone is there, without agenda, without expectation. Just there. That kind of presence is powerful. It says, "You don't have to do anything to earn my care. Your pain is safe with me." We live in a world that teaches us to compete, compare, and pretend. Social media often magnifies this illusion of perfection. We scroll through filtered lives and forget that behind every smiling photo is a silent battle, a heartbreak, a fear. What if, instead of pretending we had it all together, we started sharing the truth with one another? Imagine how many people would feel less alone, less ashamed, more alive.

Connection doesn't require you to be perfect. It requires you to be present. To show up with your messy heart, to listen deeply, to hold space when someone is falling apart not with advice, but with empathy and slowly, these moments become the glue that binds souls together. You begin to trust. You begin to soften. You begin to believe that you're not alone and maybe never were. If you've ever felt too broken for love, hear this: your cracks are not your curse; they are your connection points. The places you've been hurt most deeply are often the places where you can love others most powerfully. Because once you've walked through fire, you recognize the flames in someone else's eyes and you sit beside them, not in fear, but in solidarity. Let people in, not when you're fixed, but when you're real. Let your trembling voice speak. Let your tears fall without apology. You don't need to wait until you've "healed enough" to be worthy of companionship. Healing *is* the companionship. The shared space. The understanding gaze. The hand that doesn't pull you up but simply holds yours while you rise. You're allowed to be both a masterpiece and a work in progress, all at once. You're allowed to carry your past and still build your future and above all, you're allowed to heal in the arms of another, not despite your flaws, but because of the courage it takes to reveal them. There is a quiet ache inside every human being, the longing to be seen. Not just looked at, not merely noticed, but truly *seen*. For someone to witness your story, your soul, your fears, your little triumphs, and to say, "I see you, and you matter." This, more than any medicine, can heal wounds that years of loneliness have carved into the heart.

So many of us grow up feeling invisible in the very spaces where we should have been cherished. We perform, we achieve, we smile through pain, hoping someone will look past the surface and notice the storm behind our eyes. But often, the world rewards the mask more than the truth. And over time, we begin to doubt: *Will anyone ever see the real me? And if they do, will they stay?*

But the answer lies in this simple truth - being seen begins with *seeing.* When you start to see others, you create a mirror for yourself. When you sit with someone's sadness and don't rush to fix it, when you celebrate someone's small joys as if they were your own, when you remember details others forget - you become a healer, not just of them, but of yourself. You start to realize how much tenderness there is in the act of paying attention.

When a devotee sees the deity in a temple, and the deity "sees" the devotee back, there is a transfer of divine energy. That same energy exists in human connection too. When someone truly sees you without judgment, it's like standing in the presence of something holy. It validates your existence. It reminds you: *You are real. You are here. You matter.* Being seen doesn't always come through grand gestures. Sometimes, it's in the way someone remembers how you take your tea. It's in the quiet "Are you okay?" when your smile doesn't reach your eyes. It's in someone waiting for your answer not your polite one, but your honest one. These are the sacred moments where souls touch, where healing begins not through fixing but through presence. But there's another side to this truth. You must also dare to *let yourself be seen.* This is the hard part. Because to be seen means to be vulnerable. It means letting someone into your fears, your dreams, your pain, your weirdness, your depth. It means removing the armor and saying, "This is me. Will you stay?" And sometimes, people won't. But those who do those who see you in your rawest form and offer love instead of retreat are your sacred ones. Your safe harbors.

Let this book upto this given you a reminder that the world doesn't need a perfect version of you. It needs the *true* you. The one who cries at the little things. The one who gets nervous before speaking. The one who loves deeply, hurts often, and still hopes wildly. That version of you is already enough. That version of you deserves to be seen and to see others with the same depth and devotion. So today, pause. Look someone in the eyes. Listen without waiting to reply. Ask a deeper question. Remember a forgotten moment. Be that rare person who sees beneath the surface. And allow yourself to be seen too. For in those sacred moments of mutual visibility, you'll find what we all crave not perfection, but presence. Not attention, but understanding. There are people in this world who walk through darkness every day with no sign of light, and yet miraculously they become light for others. They smile gently while carrying invisible weights, they offer encouragement when they themselves are unsure, and they hold space for others to fall apart, even when their own soul is in shambles. These are the quiet lighthouses of the world those who shine not because they have never known darkness, but because they refused to let it consume them.

Being the light for someone else does not require perfection. It does not mean you have all the answers, or that your life is free from sorrow. Quite the opposite, it means that you've walked through shadows deep enough to understand that no one should ever feel alone in theirs. It means that your empathy is born not from sympathy, but from survival. You are the proof that a flicker of kindness can save a life, that one moment of connection can be a turning point in someone's story.

Think of the moments in your life where a single word, a kind gesture, a long-held gaze stopped you from unraveling. Maybe someone stayed when they could've walked away. Maybe they saw the pain behind your silence and chose to hold it without asking you to explain. Maybe they made you laugh when you had forgotten how to. Those moments are not small—they are sacred. They are turning points that deserve to be remembered.

And now, it is your turn to pass it on.

We often underestimate the power of our presence. We think, *Who am I to make a difference?* But let me tell you something profoundly true: You don't have to change the whole world, you only have to reach one person. Just one. And that, in itself, is a revolution. You never know who is hanging by a thread. You never know who is searching for a reason to stay. Your message, your time, your attention might be that reason. The smile you offer to a stranger, the reply you give to a friend who hasn't spoken in days, the small compliment, the shared silence, these are the unseen acts of bravery that hold humanity together.

In our Indian villages, the tradition of lighting a lamp at dusk carries a deeper meaning. It's not just about dispelling physical darkness, but about invoking warmth, hope, and the promise of tomorrow. Imagine if we lived like that—lighting lamps in the lives of those around us, not by force, but through presence. Not through speeches, but through sincerity.

To be someone's light is not to guide them out of their pain, but to walk beside them until they remember how to shine on their own and in doing so, you heal too. Every time you give hope, some of it returns to you. Every time you listen to someone else's silence, your own voice grows stronger. Every time you become a safe space for another human being, you find safety in your own existence.

So, let this page be a vow. That you will not wait to be perfect to offer your light. That you will start where you are, with what you have. That you will stop measuring your worth by how much you've achieved and start seeing it in how much light you've brought into the world. For in the end, we are remembered not by our resumes, but by how we made people feel. And if, in your lifetime, you can make even one person feel seen, safe, and significant then you have already lived a remarkable life. Compassion is a force so subtle, yet so transformative, it can alter the course of entire lives without making a single sound. It begins with a decision, an intentional choice to see others not as strangers or burdens, but as fellow travelers on this unpredictable journey called life. When you cultivate compassion within yourself, you set off ripples that extend far beyond your immediate circle, touching places and people you may never even meet.

Imagine a single drop of water falling into a still pond. The impact is tiny, but the ripples spread endlessly outward, crossing boundaries, merging with other waves, reaching distant shores. Compassion works in the same way. One act whether it is a gentle word, a helping hand, or simply a patient ear carries the potential to spread far beyond the moment it occurs. In the crowded, fast-paced world we live in, it's easy to forget the power of these small acts. Yet history is filled with stories of individuals whose simple gestures changed the lives of millions. Consider the kindness of a teacher who believed in a struggling child, the forgiveness extended by someone who chose peace over revenge, or the courage of a person who spoke out against injustice. These acts may seem minor at first glance, but they accumulate and amplify, inspiring others to act in kind.

How often do we judge ourselves harshly, dismiss our own pain, or withhold forgiveness? Self-compassion is the foundation on which all other compassion stands. It allows us to acknowledge our imperfections without shame, to heal old wounds, and to extend patience to ourselves when life feels overwhelming. When you treat yourself with the same gentleness you offer others, you become a source of strength rather than a vessel of self-criticism. Once rooted in self-compassion, your ability to empathize with others deepens. You become attuned not just to their words, but to the feelings beneath them. You learn to listen without interrupting, to hold space without rushing, and to respond with kindness even when it's difficult.

This ripple of compassion can change families, communities, and societies. It can transform conflicts into conversations, despair into hope, and isolation into connection. When one person chooses to act compassionately, they invite others to do the same, creating a wave of humanity that is both powerful and healing.

Today, I invite you to reflect on the ripples you want to create. What small acts of compassion can you offer in your daily life? How can you bring more kindness into your relationships, your workplace, and your community? Remember, the smallest gesture can have the greatest impact.

Compassion doesn't require grand gestures or perfect timing. It only asks for a willing heart and an open mind. Our society, conditioned to value strength, success, and invulnerability, tends to shy away from showing the parts of ourselves that feel fragile or exposed. Yet, true courage lies not in hiding our vulnerabilities but in embracing them fully. To be vulnerable is to be authentic, to live honestly, and to open ourselves to deeper connection and growth.

Think about the moments when you've felt most alive, when you shared a heartfelt truth, admitted a mistake, or asked for help. Those moments, though sometimes uncomfortable, are acts of bravery. They require us to risk rejection, judgment, or disappointment. But they also invite trust, empathy, and intimacy. Vulnerability is the gateway to genuine relationships because it shows others who we truly are beneath the surface.

In Indian culture, stories and teachings from ancient scriptures celebrate vulnerability as a strength. The *Bhagavad Gita* reveals that even the greatest warriors like Arjuna felt fear, doubt, and confusion before battle. The path to enlightenment is not about denying these emotions but learning to face them with courage and clarity. Similarly, saints and poets like Kabir and Mirabai expressed their deepest pains and doubts openly, inviting others to find solace and strength in shared humanity.

Vulnerability also plays a vital role in personal growth. When you allow yourself to face your fears and insecurities, you create space for healing. Pretending to be perfect or invincible traps you in isolation, preventing you from learning and evolving. But vulnerability is like opening a door once it's open, light can enter, revealing new possibilities and insights. To practice vulnerability, start with small steps. Share a feeling you've been holding back with a trusted friend. Admit when you don't know something instead of pretending otherwise. Allow yourself to cry, to pause, to simply be. These acts build emotional resilience, strengthening your ability to face life's uncertainties without armor. Remember, vulnerability is not about oversharing or becoming emotionally overwhelmed. It's about owning your story with honesty and compassion. It's about showing up as your imperfect, evolving self and inviting others to do the same. When you live vulnerably, you give permission for others to be authentic too. You create a safe space where connection blossoms, where empathy flows freely, and where healing begins. In this space, true courage is born not the absence of fear, but the willingness to face it.

So today, dare to be vulnerable. Step into your truth, even if it feels scary. You might discover that in your openness, you find a wellspring of strength you never knew existed. In a world filled with noise whether from endless notifications, rushing crowds, or our own racing thoughts truly listening has become a rare gift. Yet, compassionate listening is one of the most profound ways to become a light for others. It requires presence, patience, and a heart willing to hold space without judgment or interruption. When someone speaks to us from their pain, confusion, or joy, they are offering a piece of their soul. To listen compassionately is to honor that offering. It means setting aside distractions, quieting our inner chatter, and focusing fully on the other person's words, emotions, and silences. It's an act of kindness that says: "You matter. Your story matters."

The great Indian poet Rabindranath Tagore wrote, "Faith is the bird that feels the light when the dawn is still dark." Vulnerability is the bird that sings its song even in darkness, trusting that light will come. It is the acceptance of uncertainty and imperfection, the willingness to be seen just as you are.

Accepting vulnerability begins with self-awareness. Notice the moments when you resist sharing your true feelings. What fears arise? Fear of judgment? Rejection? Disappointment? Recognize these emotions without harshness. Then, gently challenge the stories that keep you locked behind walls.

Sharing vulnerability doesn't mean oversharing or burdening others with every detail. It means choosing authentic moments and trusted people with whom you can be real. It means saying, "I don't have it all figured out," or "I need help," or "This hurts me." Such honesty invites healing for yourself and those who hear you. When you show your vulnerabilities, you become relatable. Others see that they are not alone in their struggles. You light the path for someone else to step out of their isolation and into connection. This ripple effect strengthens communities and nurtures collective resilience. Remember, vulnerability is not a one-time act but a practice. It grows stronger the more you embrace it. Like a muscle, it strengthens through use. With time, you will notice how vulnerability empowers you to live more fully and love more deeply. Think about someone you admire deeply. Chances are, what draws you to them is not just what they say but how they live. Their courage in adversity, humility in success, or calm amidst chaos becomes a beacon that lights your own path. Leading by example means consistently showing up for yourself and others with honesty and respect. It means choosing compassion even when anger feels easier, maintaining integrity even when shortcuts tempt you, and practicing forgiveness even when hurt runs deep.

This approach requires strength - quiet, steady strength. It is not about perfection but about commitment to growth and authenticity. When you embrace your own journey with its struggles and lessons, you model resilience and hope. Others watch closely, sometimes more than you realize. Your way of handling setbacks, your generosity in daily life, your capacity to listen and support, these small acts extending, inspiring change beyond your immediate circle.

Ultimately, leading by example creates a quiet revolution. It plants seeds of light in the hearts of others, inviting them to shine in their own unique ways and when many such lights connect, darkness retreats. Leading by example is not just a moral ideal. It is deeply rooted in both psychological science and ancient wisdom traditions. Understanding why and how it influences others can empower you to consciously become that guiding light.

From a psychological perspective, humans are inherently social beings who learn primarily through observation - a process called **social learning theory**, introduced by psychologist Albert Bandura. This theory explains that people acquire new behaviors by watching others, especially those they respect or identify with. The behaviors modeled by leaders, parents, teachers, or peers become templates for others to imitate.

When you consistently exhibit positive behaviors like empathy, resilience, and ethical choices, you create a mental map in observers' minds - a "living example" that motivates and normalizes those qualities.

Conversely, inconsistency or hypocrisy breaks trust and dims your influence.

Neuroscience further supports this through the concept of **mirror neurons**, the brain cells that fire both when we act and when we witness others' actions. Mirror neurons allow us to intuitively understand emotions and intentions, fostering empathy and connection. Your calmness in crisis or generosity in daily life activates these neurons in others, creating emotional resonance and inspiring similar responses.

On the spiritual side, ancient Indian philosophies and global wisdom traditions affirm that **self-mastery** is the foundation of leadership. The Bhagavad Gita, one of India's timeless texts, speaks of the enlightened individual as one who acts without attachment to personal gain, embodying virtues naturally rather than through force.

Similarly, the Buddhist concept of **right action** (samma kammanta) encourages acting in ways that promote harmony and compassion, which then radiates outward to benefit all beings. Such teachings highlight that the true leader's power lies not in control but in becoming a living embodiment of higher values.

Real-world examples reflect this truth. Consider Mother Teresa, whose unwavering compassion drew millions to acts of kindness. Their lives demonstrated that genuine change begins within and spreads outward quietly yet irresistibly.

Yet leading by example requires profound self-awareness and humility. It means recognizing your imperfections and working continuously to align your actions with your ideals. It is a lifelong journey, not a destination. Dr. Brené Brown, a pioneering researcher on vulnerability and courage, emphasizes that vulnerability is the birthplace of **authenticity, empathy, and trust**. When you openly acknowledge your challenges, fears, or failures, you remove the distance between yourself and others. This honesty invites others to relate to you as a fellow human being, not an untouchable ideal.

Vulnerability breaks down the illusion of isolation. It reminds everyone that growth is a shared human experience. For someone trying to inspire or guide others, this creates an environment where people feel safe to be themselves, take risks, and pursue change without fear of judgment.

In spiritual teachings, vulnerability is also embraced as a path to humility and compassion. The Bhagavad

Gita encourages self-reflection and surrender, not surrender in defeat, but surrender to the flow of life's lessons, including those moments of weakness. This openness transforms personal struggles into sources of wisdom and empathy.

Consider leaders who have openly shared their own failures or mental health struggles, like Nelson Mandela or Jacinda Ardern. Their willingness to be vulnerable has deepened public trust and made their leadership more relatable and impactful. In practical terms, leading by example with vulnerability means sharing your story honestly your doubts, mistakes, and growth while maintaining your commitment to your values. It means modeling resilience not as flawless success, but as the ability to rise after falling. The power of leading by example is not just philosophical or ethical. It is deeply rooted in the biology of the human brain. Mirror neurons activate both when we perform an action and when we observe others performing the same action. This mirroring mechanism allows humans to intuitively understand others' intentions, emotions, and behaviors without verbal communication. In other words, when you lead by example, your brain directly influences others' brains through this biological resonance.

This neural mirroring forms the foundation for **social learning**, the process by which individuals learn new behaviors by observing others. It explains why people often unconsciously mimic the habits, emotional states, and attitudes of those they respect or follow. Your behavior, whether positive or negative, literally shapes how others think and act. Research using functional magnetic resonance imaging (fMRI) shows that mirror neuron systems are especially engaged when observing **authentic and emotionally expressive behavior**. This suggests that superficial or forced actions fail to create the deep neural impact needed to inspire genuine change. Authenticity enhances the brain's ability to simulate and internalize observed behaviors. Beyond mirror neurons, the brain's **reward circuits** also play a crucial role. When followers see a leader acting with integrity, courage, or kindness, their brains release dopamine, the neurotransmitter associated with motivation and pleasure. This reward response not only reinforces admiration but also increases the likelihood of emulating those behaviors.

Furthermore, the brain's **default mode network (DMN)** involved in self-referential thought and reflection engages when individuals consider the values and character of a leader. Consistent alignment between a leader's words and actions activates this network, fostering deeper cognitive and emotional integration of the leader's example. Understanding these neural dynamics highlights why leadership is more than giving instructions or issuing commands; it is a biological and psychological process of connection and transformation. The brain's wiring encourages learning through observation, making your personal example a powerful vector for change. In **classical Western philosophy**, Aristotle's concept of *ethos* highlights that character is central to persuasion. Aristotle argued in *Rhetoric* that a speaker's credibility built through virtuous behavior is essential to influence others. His emphasis on *arete* (excellence or virtue) suggests that leaders must embody the virtues they wish to cultivate in their communities. This reflects the idea that leadership is as much about being as about doing.

Meanwhile, **Confucian philosophy** in East Asia places immense importance on the moral example of rulers and elders. Confucius taught that a leader's virtue radiates like the sun, guiding society by its light. The concept of *junzi* (the "noble person") encapsulates this ideal: one who leads not through force but through personal integrity and moral rectitude. In this worldview, social harmony arises when leaders embody ethical principles visibly and consistently.

From an **Indian philosophical perspective**, the principle of *dharma* integrated with duty, righteousness, and the example set by individuals in society. The Bhagavad Gita emphasizes acting according to one's duty with selflessness and dedication, serving as an exemplar for others to follow. The idea that actions ripple outward and affect the collective consciousness reinforces the power of personal conduct in shaping societal norms.

Culturally, leading by example also intersects with the concept of **role modeling** and **social storytelling**. Many indigenous traditions pass down values and lessons through narratives about ancestors and heroes whose lives serve as living exemplars. These stories carry moral wisdom, teaching younger generations not just what to do, but how to embody virtues through concrete actions. In today's complex, multicultural world, understanding these philosophical and cultural roots enriches our appreciation of why leading by example remains vital. It connects us to ancient wisdom and timeless human truths about the nature of influence, responsibility, and collective flourishing. One of the strongest reasons leading by example matters is because it builds something we all need: trust. Trust is the invisible glue that holds relationships, teams, and communities together. When someone acts the way they say they will, people begin to believe in them.

Imagine a manager at work who always shows up on time, treats everyone fairly, and stays calm under pressure. This manager doesn't just tell their team what to do. They show it through their own behavior. Because of this, team members trust that their leader is reliable and honest. They feel safer and more motivated to do their best. Trust isn't given lightly. It grows slowly, step by step, through consistent actions. When leaders talk about values like honesty, kindness, or hard work but don't live by them, trust fades. Words without matching actions can feel empty or even dishonest.

Leading by example inspires change because it gives people a real, visible path to follow. It's one thing to hear about courage or patience. It's another to see someone facing a tough situation with calm and confidence. That example becomes a kind of map showing others what is possible.

This kind of leadership is powerful because it creates a ripple effect. When one person behaves well, others often want to follow. It's like a small light in the dark that slowly grows brighter as more people join in. Change starts with just one person willing to act differently. Moreover, leading by example builds respect naturally. People respect those who live their values rather than just preach them. This respect makes it easier to work together, solve problems, and overcome challenges.

So, the next time you want to inspire change, remember: show it first. Your actions speak louder than words. Leading by example isn't about being perfect. It's about being real, consistent, and courageous enough to do what you believe is right.

10. The Eternal Flame

When we think about living a good life, most of us imagine comfort, success, and happiness. These are important. We all want to feel safe, enjoy our work, and share joyful moments with loved ones. But there is a deeper question beneath these desires: What does it mean to live a *meaningful* life?

A meaningful life goes beyond just feeling good or achieving goals. It is about feeling that your life matters that your actions have purpose and contribute to something bigger than yourself. This idea has fascinated philosophers, psychologists, and spiritual teachers for centuries. Why do some people find deep satisfaction even through hardship? Why do others with wealth and comfort feel empty? Recent research in positive psychology offers answers. Studies show that people who live meaningful lives tend to have better mental health, stronger relationships, and greater resilience. Meaning gives us a reason to keep going when times are tough. It helps us connect with others and experience a sense of belonging. But meaning is not something you find like a hidden treasure; it's something you create, step by step. It often grows from your values those deep beliefs about what truly matters to you. When your daily actions align with your core values, your life begins to glow with a sense of purpose, like an eternal flame burning steadily inside.

This flame isn't about fame or fortune. It's about authenticity, living in a way that is true to who you are. It calls you to face life's challenges with courage and to use your unique gifts in service of others. This is what makes life not just good, but meaningful. In this chapter, we will explore how to ignite and nurture your eternal flame. We'll look at practical steps rooted in science and timeless wisdom. You'll learn how to discover your values, build habits that support purpose, and find clarity even in confusing times.

Most importantly, this chapter will push you to reflect on your own life. What is your eternal flame? How can you keep it burning bright, through both joy and struggle? How can living with meaning transform not only your own life but also the lives of those around you?

Living a meaningful life is a journey. Sometimes

challenging, often rewarding, and always worth pursuing. Together, let's take the first step toward that lasting flame. Before we can live a meaningful life, it's important to understand what meaning really means. Meaning is not just a vague feeling or a fancy word. It's a powerful force that shapes how we see the world and ourselves. Psychologists often define meaning as a sense that life is coherent, purposeful, and significant. This means three things: first, life feels understandable and makes sense; second, your actions and goals matter and fit together; third, you feel that your existence has value and importance.

Think about the last time you felt truly connected to something bigger than yourself. Maybe it was helping a friend, creating art, or being part of a community. Those moments often bring a deep sense of meaning because they remind us that we belong and contribute. Research shows that having meaning improves mental and physical health. People with a strong sense of meaning are less likely to suffer from depression and anxiety. They tend to live longer and recover faster from illness. This is because meaning gives us a reason to keep going, even when life gets hard. On the other hand, people who feel life lacks meaning often experience emptiness, loneliness, or despair. This feeling can lead to unhealthy habits or even physical illness. Meaning acts like a shield that protects us from these negative effects.

One well-known psychologist, Viktor Frankl, who survived the horrors of the Holocaust, wrote about how meaning helped him survive. He noticed that those who found purpose even in suffering - were more likely to survive and thrive. Frankl believed that meaning is the primary drive in human life, even more important than pleasure or power. So how do we find meaning? It often begins with exploring your values, the principles that guide your choices. Values might include kindness, creativity, freedom, or family. When you live in line with your values, your life feels more coherent and fulfilling. Meaning also grows when you set goals that reflect those values. For example, if you value kindness, your goal might be to help others regularly. If creativity matters to you, you might dedicate time to expressing yourself through art or writing.

This connection between values, goals, and actions creates what some call a "meaningful life cycle." Each step feeds the next, building a stronger, brighter flame inside you.Meaning is deeply personal. What matters to one person might not matter to another. That's why it's important to reflect honestly on what gives your life purpose and direction. At the center of a meaningful life are your core values, those deeply held beliefs about what is most important to you. These values act like a compass, guiding your decisions, actions, and how you relate to the world. When you live according to your values, your life feels authentic and fulfilling. Many people have never truly thought about what their values are. Instead, they live according to what others expect, what society praises, or what seems convenient at the moment. This can create a feeling of emptiness or confusion because their actions don't reflect who they really are.

Discovering your core values requires honest reflection and patience. It means asking yourself questions like: What matters most to me? What kind of person do I want to be? What brings me joy and peace? What would I stand up for, no matter what? Values can be simple but powerful. For example, kindness, honesty, courage, creativity, family, freedom, or learning. These are not just words but feelings and actions that shape your daily life. One practical way to find your values is to look back at moments when you felt truly proud or fulfilled. What was happening then? Who were you with? What actions did you take? These moments often reveal what your values are in action.

Another approach is to think about people you

admire. What qualities do they have that you respect? Sometimes, the values we admire in others reflect what we want to live by ourselves. Once you identify your values, it's important to test if they truly feel right for you. Values should inspire and motivate you, not create pressure or guilt. They should feel like a source of energy, not a heavy burden. Living according to your values means making choices that align with them, even when it's hard. For example, if honesty is a core value, you might choose to speak the truth even when it's uncomfortable. If kindness matters most, you might volunteer or support someone in need, even when you are busy. Aligning your life with your values is not about perfection. It's about making small but consistent decisions that reflect what you care about deeply. This alignment creates a sense of meaning that lights your inner flame.

Studies show that people who act in line with their values experience greater happiness, lower stress, and stronger relationships. This is because living authentically reduces inner conflict and builds trust with yourself and others. Once you have a clear sense of your core values, the next step is to turn them into practical goals. Goals act like a bridge between your inner values and the world you live in. They help you bring meaning into everyday life by giving you clear direction and motivation.

But not all goals create meaning. Some goals focus only on external success - money, status, or approval from others. These can bring temporary happiness but often leave us feeling empty once the goal is achieved. Meaningful goals, on the other hand, connect deeply with what you care about and inspire you to grow. To set meaningful goals, start by asking: How can I express my values through what I do each day? For example, if one of your values is kindness, your goal might be to volunteer regularly or to practice small acts of kindness with friends and family. If learning is a core value, you might set a goal to read a new book every month or take a course that excites you. Goals should be clear, realistic, and flexible. Life can be unpredictable, so it's important to adjust your goals as you grow and your circumstances change. What matters most is that your goals continue to reflect your values and keep your inner flame alive.

Research in psychology shows that people who set intrinsic goals those focused on personal growth, relationships, or community experience more lasting satisfaction and well-being than those who focus mainly on external rewards. These intrinsic goals help build resilience, meaning you can bounce back more easily from challenges. Sometimes, goals also need to include rest and self-care. Living a meaningful life doesn't mean constant struggle. It means balancing action with rest, ambition with peace. When you care for yourself, your flame burns brighter and longer. Meaningful goals are important, but the way to truly keep your eternal flame burning is through daily habits. Habits are the small, repeated actions that shape your life. They create the structure where your values and goals can thrive. Many people underestimate the power of habits because they seem small or ordinary. Yet, science shows that habits control about 40% of our daily actions. This means your daily habits have a huge influence on how meaningful your life feels.

Building habits that support your values creates momentum. For example, if you value health, a habit like taking a short walk every morning connects you to that value regularly. If kindness matters, a habit of sending a kind message or helping someone each day strengthens your sense of purpose. The key to building lasting habits is to start small. Trying to change everything at once often leads to frustration and giving up. Instead, pick one habit that feels doable and focus on it. For example, instead of deciding to meditate for an hour, start with just two minutes a day. Once that feels natural, you can build from there. Another important habit is reflection. Taking a few moments each day to think about how your actions matched your values helps you stay aware and intentional. This might be journaling, meditating, or simply sitting quietly before bed.

Science supports this practice. Studies show that people who reflect regularly experience greater self-awareness and emotional balance. This reflection helps you notice what's working and what needs adjustment, so your flame stays bright and steady. Environment also plays a role in habit building. Surrounding yourself with reminders of your values and goals makes it easier to stay on track. This could be photos, quotes, or even people who inspire you. Your environment shapes your habits just as much as your willpower does. It's natural to face challenges or slip-ups along the way. What matters is how you respond. Instead of harsh judgment or giving up, treat yourself with kindness. Habits grow through patience and persistence, not perfection. When your daily habits align with your values and goals, you create a life that feels meaningful every day. Your eternal flame isn't a distant idea but a living reality, glowing through your actions, thoughts, and connections. Emotions are often seen as obstacles things to control or ignore. But modern psychology shows that emotions are essential signals, like a built-in GPS for your inner world. They tell you what matters to you, what needs attention, and when you are off course. Emotional clarity means recognizing your feelings without judgment. It means being able to name what you feel, whether it's joy, sadness, anger, or fear. When you can clearly identify your emotions, you gain insight into your needs and values. For example, feeling anxious might signal that a situation conflicts with your values or that you need more preparation. Feeling joy might indicate that you are aligned with what truly matters to you. This awareness helps you make choices that keep your eternal flame burning bright. Research supports this. Studies in emotional intelligence show that people who develop emotional clarity experience less stress, better relationships, and greater overall well-being. They are better able to manage challenges and maintain motivation toward meaningful goals. It's also important to accept emotions, even difficult ones. Resistance to emotions often makes them stronger or causes avoidance behaviors. Acceptance allows you to face feelings honestly, heal from pain, and grow stronger. Emotional clarity is not about feeling happy all the time. It's about feeling real, authentic, and connected to yourself. This genuine emotional connection fuels the eternal flame with truth and resilience. In fact, emotional clarity deepens meaning by linking your inner world to your outer actions. It helps you avoid living on autopilot or chasing goals that don't fit who you are. Instead, you live intentionally, with heart and mind aligned. As you cultivate emotional clarity, you may find your relationships also improve. When you understand your feelings, you communicate more clearly and empathize better with others. This strengthens bonds and creates a supportive environment for your meaningful life. Ambition drives many of us forward. It pushes us to achieve, create, and improve. Ambition can be a powerful force for good, helping us reach our goals and live according to our values. But if left unchecked, ambition can also cause stress, burnout, and dissatisfaction. The key to living a meaningful life is balancing ambition with inner peace, keeping your eternal flame steady rather than letting it burn out. Research shows that people who manage to balance striving for success with moments of calm and contentment experience greater well-being. This balance helps us avoid extremes: neither restless chasing nor passive stagnation. Inner peace doesn't mean giving up on your dreams. Instead, it's about cultivating a calm heart that can face life's ups and downs without losing hope or direction. It's the quiet confidence that comes from knowing your purpose and trusting the process, even when things are uncertain. One practical way to balance ambition and peace is through setting boundaries. This means recognizing your limits and saying no when necessary. Boundaries protect your energy and help you focus on what truly matters. Without them, ambition can lead to overwork, exhaustion, and losing touch with your values. Balancing ambition with peace requires regular reflection. Taking time to check in with yourself and asking, "Am I pushing too hard? Am I honoring my values? Am I taking care of my well-being?" helps you adjust your pace and direction.

Remember, a steady flame burns longer than a bright, quick blaze. When ambition and peace work together, they create a rhythm of purposeful effort and restful renewal. This rhythm sustains you through life's challenges and joys. Human beings are deeply social creatures. Our relationships with family, friends, and community are among the most powerful influences on the meaning we find in life. Strong, healthy connections act like fuel for your eternal flame, giving warmth, support, and light during both easy and challenging times.

Psychological research shows that people with close relationships tend to live longer, experience less stress, and enjoy higher levels of happiness. This is because meaningful relationships fulfill basic human needs: to belong, to be understood, and to contribute to something larger than ourselves. But not all relationships nourish your flame equally. Some connections drain your energy, cause pain, or pull you away from your values. Part of living meaningfully is learning to recognize which relationships uplift you and which ones hold you back. Healthy relationships are built on trust, respect, and mutual care. They allow you to be your authentic self without fear of judgment. When you feel safe to share your thoughts and feelings, your eternal flame glows brighter.

Moreover, relationships provide opportunities for growth. They challenge you to develop empathy, patience, and forgiveness. These qualities deepen your emotional clarity and help you live with greater compassion both for yourself and others. It's important to remember that relationships require effort and attention. Like any flame, they need tending. Regular communication, active listening, and spending quality time together strengthen your bonds and create lasting meaning. In addition, giving to others like whether through kindness, support, or service amplifies your sense of purpose. When you turn your pain or struggles into acts of helping others, your flame expands beyond yourself, creating a legacy of light. Science confirms this. Studies show that volunteering or helping others increases feelings of happiness and life satisfaction. Altruism connects you to a community and reinforces your values in action. At the same time, it's essential to set healthy boundaries in relationships. Saying no when needed protects your energy and keeps your flame from burning out. Boundaries help you maintain balance between giving to others and caring for yourself. From the moment we are born, relationships shape who we are. Human beings are wired for connection, and these connections play a vital role in how meaningful our lives feel. Psychologists like Dr. John Bowlby, who developed attachment theory, found that early relationships form the foundation for emotional health throughout life. When these bonds are strong and secure, our inner flame grows steady and warm. Research by Harvard's Longitudinal Study of Adult Development, which has followed people over 80 years, confirms that the quality of our relationships is the strongest predictor of happiness and health. People with close, supportive ties tend to live longer and feel more satisfied with life, regardless of wealth or fame. In fact, social connection has been shown to reduce the risk of early death by 50%, according to a meta-analysis published in *PLoS Medicine*.

However, not all relationships are positive. Toxic relationships can drain energy and increase stress, reducing our sense of meaning. Psychologists emphasize the importance of recognizing these harmful dynamics and setting boundaries to protect your well-being. Learning to say no to relationships that undermine your values is crucial for preserving your eternal flame. Healthy relationships are built on trust, respect, and genuine care. When you feel safe being yourself, your flame glows brighter. For example, consider Malala Yousafzai, the Nobel laureate and education activist. She credits the unwavering support of her family for giving her strength to continue advocating for girls' education, despite threats and violence. This support network was vital to her resilience and sense of purpose.

Relationships also teach us important skills like empathy and forgiveness, which deepen emotional clarity and enrich our lives. When we open ourselves to others' experiences, we become more compassionate and connected, which fuels our own inner light. Moreover, acts of kindness and service in relationships amplify meaning. Studies show that volunteering and helping others activate the brain's reward system, releasing dopamine and endorphins that boost mood and well-being. When you turn your pain into service, your flame extends beyond yourself, creating a legacy of hope and light. Resilience is the ability to recover from setbacks and keep moving forward. It's like the steady fuel that keeps your eternal flame burning even when life gets hard. Everyone faces challenges like loss, failure, pain but resilient people find ways to grow stronger through these experiences. Research by Dr. Ann Masten, a leading psychologist on resilience, calls it "ordinary magic." She found that resilience is not a rare gift but a common, natural capacity that can be nurtured. It comes from protective factors like supportive relationships, positive self-belief, and the ability to manage emotions. A powerful example of resilience is the story of Oprah Winfrey. Born into poverty and facing abuse as a child, she experienced many hardships. Yet, Oprah's belief in her worth and purpose, supported by mentors and her own determination, helped her rise to become one of the world's most influential media figures. Her journey shows how resilience can turn pain into power. Building resilience starts with developing emotional clarity understanding your feelings and accepting them without judgment. This helps you face difficulties honestly rather than avoiding or denying them. Mindfulness and journaling are proven tools to cultivate this clarity. Another key factor is fostering strong connections. Having people who support and believe in you provides a safety net during tough times. Social support lowers stress and boosts recovery, according to a study in *Psychological*

Science. Resilient people also tend to reframe challenges as opportunities for learning. Instead of seeing failure as defeat, they view it as feedback and a chance to improve. Practicing gratitude is another way to build resilience. Recognizing what you still have and what's good in life creates positive emotions that buffer against stress. Studies have found that grateful people report better health, more happiness, and stronger relationships. As you nurture resilience, your eternal flame becomes brighter and more enduring. It carries you through storms and guides you toward a meaningful life filled with purpose and peace. Change is a constant in life. From childhood to adulthood, from job shifts to loss of loved ones, change shapes our journey. While many fear change because it brings uncertainty, learning to embrace it is essential for keeping your eternal flame alive and thriving.

Psychologists say that how we respond to change often determines our happiness and growth. Dr. Elisabeth Kübler-Ross's famous model of the five stages of grief shows that even difficult changes involve a process like denial, anger, bargaining, depression, and acceptance. Moving toward acceptance helps us find Research supports the idea that people who view change as an opportunity for growth, rather than a threat, tend to experience less stress and greater well-being. This mindset, known as psychological flexibility, allows you to adapt more easily and find new paths when old ones close. One way to develop this flexibility is through curiosity. When faced with change, asking "What can I learn from this?" or "How can this help me grow?" shifts your perspective from fear to possibility. Curiosity opens your mind and fuels resilience. Another helpful practice is self-care. Change can be exhausting, so it's important to nourish your body and mind through sleep, nutrition, exercise, and relaxation. Taking care of yourself strengthens your ability to adapt and keep your flame steady. Social support also plays a crucial role. Talking about your feelings with trusted friends or mentors can provide comfort and new insights. Shared experiences remind you that you are not alone in facing change. Spiritual or philosophical beliefs can offer additional strength. Many find comfort in faith or mindfulness practices that remind them of life's bigger picture and the flow of change as part of a greater cycle.

Remember, every ending holds a new beginning. When you embrace change rather than resist it, you invite renewal and growth. Your eternal flame shines not just because of what you hold on to, but also because of your courage to let go and move forward. Gratitude is more than just saying "thank you." It is a deep, conscious appreciation for the good things in life, big or small. This simple yet profound practice has been shown by numerous scientific studies to improve mental health, increase happiness, and deepen our sense of meaning.

Research from Dr. Robert Emmons, one of the world's leading gratitude researchers, reveals that people who regularly practice gratitude experience lower levels of stress and depression. They also report feeling more connected to others and more satisfied with life. Gratitude changes the way our brain works, encouraging us to focus on what we have rather than what we lack. Gratitude creates a positive cycle. When you appreciate the good in your life, you naturally feel more hopeful and motivated. This lifts your eternal flame higher, making it easier to face challenges and setbacks with courage. Practicing gratitude can be simple. You might start by keeping a daily journal, writing down three things you are thankful for each day. These don't have to be big events; even a kind word from a stranger or a beautiful sunset can spark gratitude. Over time, this habit rewires your brain to notice positivity more naturally. Gratitude also strengthens relationships. When you express appreciation to others, it deepens trust and connection. People feel valued and more likely to support you in return, creating a supportive community around your flame. Importantly, gratitude helps balance ambition and peace. While striving for goals, it keeps you grounded in the present, reminding you of the journey, not just the destination. This balance enriches your life with both hope for the future and joy in the now.

Research from psychologists like Dr. Emily Smith, author of *The Power of Meaning*, shows that people with a strong sense of purpose experience better mental and physical health, greater resilience, and longer lives. Purpose fuels motivation, giving you energy even when tasks feel difficult or tedious. What makes purpose so powerful is its connection to identity. When you live purposefully, you feel you are being true to who you really are. This authenticity lights up your inner flame and creates a deep sense of satisfaction. Purpose doesn't have to be grand or world-changing. It can be as simple as caring deeply for your family, creating art, or helping others in small ways. What matters is that your actions reflect what you value most. Finding your purpose often requires reflection and exploration. Questions like "What matters most to me?" or "What legacy do I want to leave?" can guide your search. Journaling, meditation, or talking with trusted friends can also reveal clues about your true calling. Living purposefully also means embracing small daily rituals that connect you to your values. This might be spending quiet moments in nature, practicing kindness, or dedicating time to a craft or hobby. These moments build momentum and keep your eternal flame glowing bright. Science backs the importance of these rituals. Studies find that routines centered around meaningful activities increase happiness and reduce anxiety. Rituals create a sense of control and continuity, especially during uncertain times. Purpose also acts as a compass during setbacks. When faced with difficulties, people anchored by purpose are more likely to adapt and keep moving forward. Their flame endures because it is fueled by something larger than immediate circumstances. Hope is often described as a light in the darkness, a quiet but powerful force that helps us endure challenges and believe in a better future. It is not wishful thinking or blind optimism; rather, hope is a realistic and active mindset rooted in the belief that change and growth are possible. Scientific studies show that hope has tangible benefits for mental and physical health. Psychologists define hope as consisting of two parts: goals (the things you want to achieve) and pathways (the routes you believe you can take to reach those goals). This combination fuels motivation and persistence, even when obstacles arise. Hope also serves as a protective factor against despair and depression. Research indicates that people with higher levels of hope cope better with chronic illness, trauma, and loss. Hope activates the brain's reward systems, releasing dopamine and helping regulate emotions. Cultivating hope starts with setting meaningful goals that inspire you. These goals give direction to your eternal flame, preventing it from flickering aimlessly. Breaking big goals into smaller, manageable steps builds confidence and reinforces your belief in progress. Equally important is cultivating flexible thinking, being willing to adjust your plans and find alternative pathways when faced with setbacks. This adaptability strengthens hope because it acknowledges challenges without giving in to defeat. Another powerful way to nurture hope is through stories and role models. Hearing about others who have overcome adversity reminds us that transformation is possible. Community support and shared experiences also reinforce hope by creating connection and belonging. Mindfulness and gratitude practices further support hope by grounding you in the present and reminding you of the resources you already have. When you focus on strengths rather than weaknesses, your flame brightens with renewed energy. Compassion is a powerful force that softens the heart and opens the door to healing. It involves feeling empathy for the suffering of others, ourselves and responding with kindness and understanding. Compassion fuels the eternal flame by deepening our connection with ourselves and the world around us. Scientific studies reveal that compassion has significant benefits for mental and physical health. Neuroscientists have found that practicing compassion activates areas of the brain associated with love and caregiving. This response reduces stress, lowers blood pressure, and even boosts the immune system. One inspiring example is the work of Fred Rogers, the beloved host of *Mister Rogers' Neighborhood*. Known for his gentle and compassionate nature, Fred Rogers dedicated his life to nurturing kindness and understanding in children. His calm presence and empathy helped millions of viewers feel seen and valued. His life shows how compassion can create ripples of healing far beyond individual moments. Many of us are our own harshest critics, especially during failure or pain. But treating ourselves with the same kindness we offer others is essential for emotional healing. Psychologist Kristin Neff's research on self-compassion shows it reduces anxiety and depression and improves motivation and resilience. Practicing compassion starts with awareness recognizing when we or others are suffering without turning away or judging. Mindfulness exercises can help develop this awareness by training the mind to stay present and open-hearted.

Acts of compassion, whether small or large, build connection. Simple gestures like listening deeply, offering a smile, or helping someone in need strengthen bonds and remind us of our shared humanity. These connections nurture our eternal flame by creating a sense of belonging and purpose. Compassion also challenges us to forgive both ourselves and others. Forgiveness frees us from the heavy burden of anger and resentment, allowing peace to settle in our hearts. Studies show that forgiveness improves emotional well-being and even physical health. Importantly, compassion fuels service. When we turn our pain into helping others, our flame grows into a beacon of hope. Volunteerism and altruistic acts trigger the brain's reward system, creating feelings of joy and fulfillment. Gratitude and generosity are like twin flames that brighten your life and the lives of others. When you cultivate gratitude, you recognize the gifts in your life, and generosity is the natural response sharing those gifts to spread light beyond yourself.

Scientific research confirms that gratitude and generosity create a powerful feedback loop, strengthening mental health, relationships, and overall well-being. Dr. Martin Seligman, a pioneer of positive psychology, found that practicing gratitude improves happiness and reduces depression.

Practicing gratitude begins with simple daily reflections. Noticing even small blessings a kind word, a safe place to sleep, fresh air grounds you in appreciation. This shifts your focus from scarcity to abundance, lighting your inner flame with positivity. Generosity extends beyond money or possessions. Time, attention, and kindness are equally valuable gifts. Volunteering, mentoring, or simply listening with full presence are acts of generosity that nourish your soul and strengthen your connections. Research shows that generous people tend to live longer, healthier lives. A 2013 study published in *Health Psychology* found that individuals who volunteered regularly had lower blood pressure and reduced risk of mortality. This demonstrates how generosity not only uplifts others but also sustains your eternal flame. Generosity also expands your sense of purpose. When you contribute to others' well-being, you connect to something larger than yourself. This connection enhances your meaning in life and deepens your fulfillment. Importantly, generosity teaches humility and gratitude for what we have. It reminds us that no matter our circumstances, we can always give in some way. This mindset dissolves fear and selfishness, allowing your flame to grow brighter and more generous. In practical terms, you might start by identifying small ways to give each day whether through a compliment, sharing knowledge, or supporting a cause. These small sparks of generosity can light a larger fire in your community and beyond. Courage is the spark that keeps your eternal flame alive when fear tries to snuff it out. It is not the absence of fear, but the choice to move forward despite it. Courage enables you to face uncertainty, failure, and pain while still pursuing a meaningful life.

Research in psychology highlights that courage is a skill that can be cultivated. It involves emotional regulation managing anxiety and doubt and cognitive flexibility,History offers many inspiring examples of courage fueling change. Everyday courage, however, looks different. It might mean speaking up for yourself, making a difficult decision, or stepping into the unknown with hope. These small acts add up, gradually building confidence and resilience. Courage also connects deeply with purpose. When your actions are aligned with your values, it becomes easier to face fear because your "why" is bigger than your doubts. Purpose gives your flame a steady fuel, even in the darkest moments. Moreover, courage fosters growth. Psychologist Carol Dweck's research on growth mindset reveals that embracing challenges rather than avoiding them leads to learning and success. Courage helps you adopt this mindset by shifting your relationship with failure from a source of shame to an opportunity for growth. Social support also fuels resilience. Humans are wired for connection, and having trusted relationships provides emotional safety and practical help during tough times. Sharing your struggles doesn't show weakness; it builds your strength. Physical health plays a surprising role too. Regular exercise, good nutrition, and sleep help regulate mood and energy, giving you the stamina to face life's challenges. Resilience is not about going it alone. It's about knowing when to reach out and accepting that healing is a journey. Each step forward, no matter how small, adds fuel to your eternal flame. Imagine standing at the edge of a vast forest. The path ahead twists and turns unpredictably, just like life itself. You can't see what's around the next bend, but you carry a small lantern in your hand, your eternal flame. Now, what if I told you that the way to keep this lantern glowing bright, no matter what you face, is by simply learning to pay attention? This is the essence of mindfulness. Take the story of Tara Brach, a psychologist and meditation teacher, who shares about a moment when she faced a wave of panic during a public talk. Instead of pushing it away, she paused, focused on her breath, and observed the panic like a curious observer. This simple act of mindfulness transformed the experience, calming her fear and allowing her to continue. Her story shows how mindfulness can protect and nourish your eternal flame in real life.

Mindfulness deepens your resilience by helping you step back from automatic reactions and choose your response. It also enhances compassion, when you see your own suffering clearly, you are more likely to treat yourself kindly. And it fuels courage by creating a stable inner space where fear can be held gently instead of controlling you. Research shows that love and connection are essential to human survival. The Harvard Study of Adult Development, one of the longest studies on happiness, found that close relationships are the strongest predictor of a long, fulfilling life. People who feel loved and connected have lower stress levels, stronger immune systems, and greater emotional resilience. But love begins within. Self-love is the practice of accepting and caring for yourself just as you are flaws, mistakes, and all. Dr. Kristin Neff, a pioneer in self-compassion research, explains that self-love reduces anxiety and helps people face challenges with greater confidence. It's not about narcissism but about a deep kindness that fuels your inner strength. Consider the story of Maya Angelou, who faced tremendous hardships in her early life but cultivated a fierce love for herself and others. Her poetry and life work demonstrate how love can be a revolutionary force, a light that inspires others to rise and shine. Love also transforms your relationships. When you approach others with genuine care and empathy, you create bonds that sustain and uplift. Neuroscience reveals that acts of love and kindness release oxytocin, sometimes called the "bonding hormone," which promotes feelings of trust and safety. Importantly, love encourages forgiveness both for yourself and those who hurt you. Forgiveness frees your heart from bitterness and opens space for healing. This release is vital for keeping your eternal flame alive and growing. Love fuels purpose. When your actions are guided by love whether through family, community, or a cause you connect to a force greater than yourself. This connection gives meaning to your journey and sustains your flame through challenges. Practicing love daily can be simple yet powerful: a kind word, a moment of patience, or a gentle touch. These small gestures accumulate, creating warmth that spreads beyond you. Ultimately, love invites you to live fully and fearlessly, knowing that your eternal flame is held in a cradle of warmth that no hardship can extinguish. First, it's essential to understand what makes this flame so powerful. Your eternal flame is born from the deepest parts of your being: your values, your passions, your experiences, and your choices. It is the fusion of your unique gifts and the meaning you create through living them.

But the flame is also fragile. It can flicker when faced with hardship, self-doubt, or disconnection. This is why every chapter of this book has focused on the essential elements that nourish and protect your flame: courage, resilience, compassion, mindfulness, gratitude, generosity, and love. Together, these form a foundation sturdy enough to withstand life's storms and flexible enough to allow growth. No journey worth taking is without its shadows. Your eternal flame shines brightest not despite the darkness, but because of it. Pain, failure, and loss are not signs that your flame is weak, they are invitations to deepen your understanding and expand your light. The Japanese art of Kintsugi, where broken pottery is repaired with gold. Instead of hiding the cracks, the gold highlights them, making the piece more beautiful and valuable. Your challenges are the gold of your soul, making your flame richer and more radiant. When you meet your pain with courage and compassion, you transform it into wisdom. When you hold yourself gently in times of struggle, you foster resilience. When you choose to love despite fear, your flame blazes with authenticity. The eternal flame is not a one-time achievement; it is a daily practice. It asks you to show up, again and again, with intention. How you choose to spend your time, where you direct your energy, and how you connect with others are all acts that feed your flame. Your eternal flame does not burn in isolation. We are social beings, wired for connection and belonging. Surround yourself with people who nourish your flame those who encourage your growth, listen deeply, and celebrate your light.

At the same time, be a flame for others. Your courage, kindness, and generosity inspire those around you. The legacy you build is not only about what you achieve but also about how you lift others to shine.

Practical Steps to Keep Your Flame Bright

Cultivate Daily Mindfulness: Spend at least five minutes a day in mindful breathing or meditation to stay grounded.

Practice Self-Compassion: When you falter, speak kindly to yourself and remember that imperfection is part of growth.

Embrace Challenges: See setbacks as opportunities to strengthen your resilience and deepen your wisdom.

Nurture Relationships: Connect regularly with loved ones and seek out communities that align with your values.

Give Generously: Offer your time, attention, or resources without expecting anything in return.

Reflect on Your Purpose: Regularly revisit what matters most to you and align your actions accordingly.

Celebrate Progress: Acknowledge every small victory and growth moment, they are the fuel for your eternal flame.

Your eternal flame is uniquely yours, a light that no one else can carry in the same way. It is a force of transformation, hope, and love. Life will challenge you, but within you lies the power to keep this flame burning bright, no matter what. Nurture it with courage, compassion, and presence. Let it guide your path, inspire others, and create a legacy far beyond yourself.

Live not just a good life, but a meaningful one. Keep your flame alive, and the world will be brighter.

Epilogue

If you are here, reading these final words, I want you to pause. Just for a moment. Close your eyes, if you can, and take a deep breath. Not because I ask you to but because you have earned it. You've traveled through these pages not as a reader, but as a quiet companion walking beside your own soul. And whether you believe it or not, something inside you has changed.

Maybe it was subtle - a line you underlined, a sentence that echoed louder than the rest, a story that felt too close to your own. Maybe it was a moment where you suddenly felt less alone. Or maybe... just maybe... it was the first time in a long time that you didn't feel the need to hide from yourself. That matters. That's enough. And that is becoming.

You see, becoming is not some grand arrival where the pain disappears and the applause begins. It's not about fixing all your flaws or forcing positivity into your wounds. Becoming is slower, softer, and often invisible to others. It's in the way you speak to yourself after making a mistake. It's in choosing to rest without guilt, to breathe through your anxiety, to forgive someone without waiting for an apology. It's in those quiet decisions that no one sees, but your soul remembers.

The world may keep rushing. People might continue measuring success by speed and noise and shiny results. But not you. Not anymore. You've learned something sacred through this journey **that real strength doesn't come from becoming someone else. It comes from finally allowing yourself to be who you are.**

There will be days after this when you will feel lost again. Days when your old doubts return, when your heart feels too heavy, when your light feels like it's fading. But now, you carry something deeper: the truth that your pain has shaped your wisdom, your silence has deepened your voice, and your wounds have made space for others to feel seen. You've become your own guide, your own comfort, your own safe place.

This book may end here, but the journey it began inside you does not. These pages were not a solution; they were a spark. A beginning. A space where your fears were allowed to rest and your strength could slowly rise. Take this with you. Take it into your relationships, your work, your art, your healing. And when someone one day stumbles under the same weight you once carried, perhaps you'll hand them this book not because it saved you, but because it reminded you that you were never truly broken.

If this book helped you remember even one forgotten part of yourself... if it sat beside you in a silent moment when no one else could... then it has served its purpose.

And when the noise gets loud again, as it surely will, just come back to yourself. Come back to your breath. Come back to the truth you now hold:

The light inside you never really leaves. It flickers. It fades. But it waits. Always and now, you know how to find it again.